FIVE MINUTES TO ETERNITY

❧

JON SMITH

WESTBOW
PRESS®
A DIVISION OF THOMAS NELSON
& ZONDERVAN

WestBow Press books may be ordered through booksellers or by contacting:

WestBow Press
A Division of Thomas Nelson & Zondervan
1663 Liberty Drive
Bloomington, IN 47403
www.westbowpress.com
844-714-3454

Scripture taken from the New King James Version®. Copyright © 1982 by Thomas Nelson. Used by permission. All rights reserved.

ISBN: 978-1-6642-2867-2 (sc)
ISBN: 978-1-6642-2869-6 (hc)
ISBN: 978-1-6642-2868-9 (e)

Library of Congress Control Number: 2021906092

Print information available on the last page.

WestBow Press rev. date: 09/15/2021

The Lifestory is an oral tradition of Jesus Christ for all the families of the earth.

To those who gave their lives in Kashmir
so others could hear the Gospel.

We commend your sacrifice to the Lord in memory of your
passion and dedication, and we commit ourselves to care for your
families and pray for continuation of the effect of your actions
and success over the force of evil that all may hear and respond
to the scriptures with a positive answer to receive redemption
and eternal life through the blood of the living Jesus Christ.

CONTENTS

Acknowledgments

All scripture quoted in this book comes from the New King James Version (NKJV) of the Bible. Copyright Thomas Nelsen 1982. Used by permission.

Credit must first go to the dear people of Kashmir, who worked out their salvation in front of us, especially those who died introducing souls to Jesus, and to who sacrificed to make this book possible by accurately reporting the details recounted herein.

Thanks also to the wonderful prayer team that has been with us: Chester, Jan and Jill, Larry, Lexi, Marc, Jane and Gail, Dennis, Stephen, Steve, Tom, Russel, Patricia, Jan, Nancy, Segran, Ferdie and Joy, Abe, Bruce, and many others among their stations in the United States, India, Malaysia, Borneo, the Philippines, and Mongolia. They uphold us at all times and have agreed with the Lord to keep us in God's plan to introduce the lost to Jesus Christ. Also, we credit David and Cheryl Kennedy, Paul and Brenda Smith, Paul and Rosa Smith, Peter and Sandra Smith, and Ann L. Smith for their prayers and their witness of this production.

I express my deep gratitude for my dear wife, Jerri. Her steadfast love, prayer, and devotion to the Lord have made possible this book and everything to do with the Lifestory.

To our blessed saviour, the Lord Jesus Christ, for His patience and His great love for all of us.

This is a special Bible verse that helps us pray for more laborers for the harvest: 2 Timothy 2:2: "And the things that you have heard from me among many witnesses, commit these to faithful men wo will be able to teach others also."

INTRODUCTION

There are many bitter divisions in the world about religions. These are sometimes stumbling blocks for those who wish to bring the most important things from God to the people. God is wise, and He has given us all the answers in His Word on how to overcome these divisions and all other blockages that keep people from His love and salvation. Our goal is simple: with love and respect, invite all persons to follow Jesus Christ. The Lifestory is an oral tradition of Jesus for all the families of the earth.

We work to bless disciples with a tool that will help open the door to access their future as Servants for the harvest. It is a gift for disciples to quickly get into live dialogue with people for the purpose of bringing each person to an opportunity to say yes or no to accepting Christ as their saviour

The Israelites and Samaritans were bitterly divided. Religious practices had become a source of conflict. One of the questions that held them apart was whether God be worshiped in Jerusalem or on a mountain in Samaria. One Samaritan is quoted in John 4:20: "Our fathers worshipped on this mountain; and you Jews say, that in Jerusalem is the place where one ought to worship."

Even with staunch divisions facing them, Jesus's disciples viewed something in this scene that may help us understand that communities of all faiths can heartily agree that the infusion of Christ brought by familiar souls with a clear, short message as a primary introduction to the Lord will cause a rapid change of heart in a community with cultural and traditional differences other than the disciples who come to share the good news. When we tell them the truth about Him from His word, He speaks to their hearts immediately, like He did in Sychar.

With the Lifestory, we strive to pass on the calling of Christ through local people into their own cultural setting without disabling their relationships and encouraging them into becoming laborers who are personally sharing with them and following Jesus. He allows the passage of authority to them as they grow in grace. Accordingly, Paul mentions this in 2 Timothy 2:2: "And the things that you have heard from me among many witnesses, commit these to faithful men who will be able to teach others also."

Jesus's disciples felt so uneasy in Sychar, Samaria, that they stayed together as they went into the village, as it is recorded in John 4:8: "For his disciples had gone away into the city to buy food." Perhaps they were more concerned about security and eating than about what status did the citizens of Sychar have with God. At the same time, Jesus was doing something quite different from them. He started live dialogue with a local person, and from the narrative it appears His dialogue contained a goal for her to come to know Him. Consider John 4:10: "Jesus answered and said to her, 'If you knew the gift of God, and who it is who says to you give me a drink; you would have asked Him, and He would have given you living water.'"

We viewed the entire conversation John recorded with Jesus and the woman at the well. When repeated, it comes to less than five minutes. It is likely to have been longer than that, but it does seem to be a relatively short time. The Sycharian woman had lots of hang-ups concerning the Jews, yet she was talking to a Jew and then became so convinced of His message that she went directly back to town without her waterpot to urge the men of Sychar to come hear Him.

Within two days of hearing Jesus, the people of Sychar came to know Him as saviour of the world, according to John 4:42: "Then they said to the woman: 'Now we believe, not because of what you said, for we ourselves have heard Him, and we know that this is indeed the Christ, the Saviour of the world.'"

Because of Christ's focus on the women, many in the city sought to hear Him. It is told in John 4:39: "And many of the Samaritans of that city believed in Him because of the word of the woman who testified, 'He told me all that I ever did.'"

In present-day Sychar, Lifestory tellers would approach the first person available and share the story and introduce them to Jesus.

When these souls having been born again and have Him in their hearts, the tellers encourage them to share Jesus with others. This will be done usually after a short training is given on how to present the Lifestory.

Our goal for how many we will harvest is always the same: 100 percent. We focus on this target like archers, keeping in mind that the Lord wants all to come to repentance. We focus on 2 Peter 3:9: "The Lord is not slack concerning His promise, as some count slackness, but is longsuffering toward us, not willing that any should perish but that all should come to repentance."

The Lifestory is a gift to help disciples engage in immediate dialogue with people for the purpose of bringing each person to Christ. This helps us achieve our goal of building up local people to be positive laborers for the harvest.

Lost souls are the harvest and are of great value, according to Mathew 16:26: "For what profit is it to a man if he gains the whole world, and loses his own soul? Or what will a man give in exchange for his soul?"

Everyone deserves an invitation to follow Jesus. Yet most people alive today will die without receiving such a direct invitation or even a clear presentation of the Gospel. This is true even in lands where many already identify with Jesus.

It is good to remember Jesus is in the middle of our witness. Consider John 12:32: "And I, if I am lifted up from the earth, I will draw all peoples to Myself."

Great things are coming. For encouragement, hear that God will fulfil His promise to bless all the families of earth in Genesis 12:3: "I will bless those who will bless you and will curse him who will curses you; and in you all the families of the earth shall be blessed."

We follow Jesus like other disciples follow Him. Jesus led Jon and Jerri Smith into a place where laborers are scarce. They are disciples because of their fruit, as it says in John 15:8. "By this my Father is glorified, that you bear much fruit; so you will be my disciples."

Prologue

Surely there was a village nearby.

"Stop!"

Without warning, three armed men suddenly appeared in front of the two young Lifestory tellers.

"Who are you, and what are you doing here?"

"We are teachers, sir," Asgat replied, humbly but clearly.

"We don't want any teachers. Go away, or we will kill you!"

"Wait," Asgat said. "If you have children, we have a story for them."

"What kind of story?"

"A beautiful story about God."

All was quiet as the elders stared at the young men.

"You may come to our school and tell the children the story, but then you must leave immediately after."

Asgat and Alifaz smiled and gave a customary greeting.

Soon many households in this village had heard about Jesus for the first time and said yes to following Him. God did several miracles that day in that large village.

But how did the Gospel get to this remote part of the Himalayas?

BEFORE THE LIFESTORY

Some of their experiences leading up to God entrusting them with the Lifestory helped to propel them to seek a better way to share the gospel with those who may have difficulties because of Cultural, ideological, or religious differences.

New Workers in a New Land

Jon and Jerri first visited Pakistan in 2006. It is a land of extremes. The Gilgit-Baltistan region of Pakistan is formally the Northern Territory.

The Northern Area is unique for having mountain ranges among the highest in the world. Imagine entering the area in an airliner at thirty thousand feet. It's amazing to see white clouds a way under twenty thousand feet with mountain tops piercing upwards into the clear blue sky.

Questions crowded into my mind as the scene below became a memory. What kind of people would live in such a place? Would they be fierce and dangerous and unpredictable? Would they have hate and distrust, and would it be a struggle to overcome? Would we learn to accept each other? Would God make a way for us to adopt the way to give the message so they can know Christ?

Jerri and I lived in these mountain areas long enough for God to affirm His call within our hearts to share His blessing in Jesus with the "children of Ishmael."

Everywhere we went, we received kindness and affection. We also noticed great differences in the kind of food they ate and the way they ate it.

For example, butter was so highly esteemed that it was traditionally present in every part of a person's life. A constant flow of ice water was used to preserve it. To celebrate a birth, a large portion of butter was prepared. Some would be eaten immediately, then the rest saved for future celebrations in that person's life, such as marriage or death. We discovered that the older the butter was the stronger it was flavoured. We could hardly swallow the butter at a funeral!

We began with a world of strangers that soon transformed into lots of friends because they respected our trust in Jesus.

Some things were difficult along the way, especially when we first arrived in Pakistan. But the days passed, as did the trials. And Jesus stayed with Jerri and me, encouraging us to keep pressing onward.

Our first place to stay in the Northern Areas of Pakistan was in Gilgit. We stayed with our wonderful friends, who were leaders in our team. Their house had cement walls and a few small windows, and it was during the cold season. We faced cultural and language barriers and we attempted to learn and be helpful to the leaders. Most of the time was spent in our small room. We wanted to get out and look around and get familiar with some of the places and people, but the leaders considered it too much of a risk.

Then it happened that Jerri became very ill. In the little room with a small window and a cold cement floor, I went to prayer on my knees. I expressed my great concern, and the leaders called a nurse friend who we will never forget. We called her Dr. Laura. In her past life, she was an army field nurse in war torn Iraq. She quickly set up an intravenous feed to rehydrate Jerri. The liquid had been near the floor and was too cold. Jerri went into shock, and we almost lost her. I cried out, and the Lord heard my prayer. Thank you, Lord! She survived.

We still love Laura to this day. What a wonderful, courageous person with a great testimony for Christ that her and all her family were to the Gilgit area.

Because of my work experience as an engineering contractor, we accepted an invitation to help construct about thirty miles of a road reaching from the high village of Hispar to the lower Himalayan town of Hunza. It was an accomplishment just to reach the village of Hispar because it required driving over treacherous roads and five rope bridges hanging high above a gorge.

Our driver, Farook, had nerves of steel. He knew that the 2005 earthquake had resulted in many large cracks in the foundations and footings of these bridges, and as far as anyone knew this would be the first Jeep over them since the earthquake.

I felt dizzy in the back of the Jeep and was thankful they halted for a break. My stomach was churning, and one way or the other I needed to be outside the vehicle. The door opened on the downside, and the sight below was awesome. I kept one hand of the Jeep as I went directly to the back. There were two women inside. One was my wife, Jerri. I hoped to be out of sight, as it would embarrass me to lose control. I reached over to the spare tire mounted on the back. I clutched it and looked down. My feet were literally at the edge of the abyss.

I noticed the driver coming back, and my head was swirling as he approached me. In Urdu he said, "Here, take and drink."

I obeyed and drank from the liter of water. Things got better because drinking lots of water is the right thing to do to overcome altitude sickness. I found my symptoms were normal for many people at this height because we were above ten thousand feet. I had it, and it stayed until we finished the trip, but drinking lots of water made it bearable.

Muslim men saw my fear of heights and prayed for me to return safely.

We had many concerns about returning to Hispar to stay, beginning with the monumental challenge of adapting to this very different way of life. It would take everything we had and more to live out the Gospel in this place. Our five children were grown, and grandchildren were arriving. We would surely miss each other. We were determined to bring a message of hope to this area, yet we needed to hear clearly from God before taking our next step in this direction.

We traveled back and forth from Islamabad to Gilgit on the amazing road called the Karakorum Highway that is often referred to as the eighth wonder of the world. It was chiselled out of solid rock.

Far below, the muddy Indus River was an angry churning snake. Every oncoming vehicle was a challenge to meet and get by safely. It would take fifteen hours for our bus to take us to Islamabad for our departure back to the States. And it seemed at least half the drive consisted of precarious stretches of highway.

On this day, I was under great stress from the bus ride, and I asked Jesus to answer a question with a simple yes or no: Should we stay in the Pakistan frontier? More precisely, I asked Him to write a yes or no on the front of the bus inside on the window.

I reasoned that He had written on the wall for someone before, so why not now while this bus was careening around curves high up on the face of a cliff? We could die at any moment, so what would it hurt to ask?

No words appeared, but to my utter surprise a memory flashed before my mind's eye of an event that had happened a few years earlier, when Jerri and I had attended a gathering in Arizona. In a time of prayer, hundreds of papers were passed out, each describing a people group who had not received a clear presentation of Jesus nor the opportunity to respond to His message of saving grace. We took one page about a people group home in America and put it on the fridge for several months and prayed for the people group they had given to us. We lost the list while moving to Pakistan. Just that moment, as I waited for the yes or no to appear on the front of the bus. Jesus did not have to write anything. He just refreshed my memory. The people group we were to pray for came as a random paper of over 600 random papers of people groups and ours was the Burusho people. I never remembered this until that moment.

A friend from Switzerland who shared my desire to introduce people to Jesus was asleep beside me, so I shook him and told him about the event. He did not understand. No matter. I understood.

Eventually, the bus stopped. My friend awoke and went to the front. In my fear of heights, I was still focusing on the rock wall on the right side. My friend shouted something at the driver, who responded with something similar. The bus soon lurched in reverse for a moment.

I glanced to the left. All I could see out of that side of the bus was air. I asked Jesus to still my heart. I did not even try to think of why we had stopped. Finally, we continued onward to Islamabad.

The peace that came from knowing the Lord had a certain plan for us made our journey much more tolerable. I had asked a question, and Jesus had answered. This was a milestone, knowing we were on track to return to Pakistan. More and more, we realized that He was holding us in His hands.

This event taught me to rely on what Jesus has already done in my life rather than asking for a sign. The rest of the trip was unnerving and challenging, but challenging was not a good reason to stay home and not come and witness the Gospel to these people.

The Burusho, also known as the Hunza or Botraj, live in Hunza, Nagar, Chitral, and in the valleys of Gilgit Baltistan in northern Pakistan as well as in Jammu and Kashmir, India. Many are Ismaili Muslim.
Burusho means "Smith," and they are known to be skilled in making and repairing tools.

LOVE THY NEIGHBOR

Jon and Jerri loved Gilgit, and they won some of their neighbours to Jesus, but they left only few elsewhere in the area who accepted Him as saviour.

Their next door neighbour was Ahamad and Soni. They had ten children. The children were mostly teenagers, and some over twenty. Jon helped with their garden by pulling weeds and turning the soil.

Both Jon and Jerri were asking God how will they come to know Christ? I had this same question every day. This day was beginning to unfold in a very different way.

Ahamad asked me to set at a wooden table centered among the flowers in the back yard. He looked across the table to me and I could tell he wanted to talk to me about something important because he kept looking me right in the face. One daughter brought a plate of sliced apples and two classes of warm buttermilk. I thought there was some sort of collaboration going on because no one was saying anything or asking if I would like this or that. Everything was just happening without requests, and it seemed like something was up. I thought this might be important. My feet were on the grass and the bench was sturdy and I felt calm as I looked back into his eyes, but there was still the question in my mind of what is he about to tell me?

These words came from his mouth: "Next week my daughter will be married to a man from Iran who his highly respected and you will be there." I simply said: "Sure why not, no problem, I will be there." I thought to myself that this is what I get for pulling weeds and digging in the garden for months. I am not a friend anymore; I am family.

A week later we entered the marriage hall then gathered with all the men and entered a large room with windows and curtains. This was my first experience at an Asian wedding. The rugs we sat on were as comfortable as the cement floor. My legs were a bit stiff, but I was able to bend them under me. Instead of being placed on a table, the dishes of food were placed on a tapestry on the floor in front of us.

When it came time we bent forward to eat or drink. To eat, we placed our left hand behind our back while grasping food with our fingertips of our right hands. Our thumb had to be held back for rice, then straightened to push it out of our palm and forward to our mouths. Once it reached our mouth we used this flipping kind of action to propel the rice deeper into our mouth. I have not mastered this technique to this day.

Each of us were given a glass of cold water. Waiters would come now and then and refill the glasses. Conversational chatter filled the room, then it was stopped for introductions. I was glad that I wasn't first, because I am a little shy in public, especially with strangers.

Ahmed's son in law to be is a bright young man in a perfect white *shavakami*. He sat on the floor next to me and introduced me to the men circled around the perimeter of the room and asked me where I was from. I said: "(*Mey Amerika se hun*) I am from America." This was all the sixty some men needed to hear. After I said this, they immediately began to ask me question after question. With each person's question, the topic became more difficult.

I found myself trying to get off the hook without refusing to try and answer. One fellow dressed in all white said this: "Did you vote for President Bush?" The next man cleared his voice and gained attention then said: "Why is America the only country in the world to drop an atomic bomb on another country?" I wasn't sweating. It was too cold for that, but I did begin to feel cornered as these questions became more like an inquisition. I was secretly hoping I could share with them an invitation to follow Jesus, but it became less likely as we went on. I think Ahmed was hoping for the same thing and he may be concerned for the salvation of his future son in law and possibly future grandchildren.

Under my breath, I called on the Lord for help.

My next statement went something like this:

"In America, we are democratic. We get a choice to vote on things like this." I noticed several men nodding their heads in agreement and I continued my reply: "I did not vote for dropping an atomic bomb on Japan. Not that I could have, but I didn't. I have found through Jesus that we only love God as much as we love the person that we hate the most." It was mostly silent, but I heard several gasps, then silence, and no more questions. Now I wish I could have had the Lifestory at that time.

Jon and Jerri lived very close to Ahamad and nearly a month later there had been friction between Jon and Jerri with some words spoken harshly and loud enough that Ahamad and Soni could hear. Ahamad came to Jon privately over a cup of tea and said: "When there is tension your wife needs to tell you how it is so you feel it. My wife is the same." After this move by Ahamad Jon and Jerri felt more secure and accepted, and later became more like family than close friends. Jerri loved Soni so much that

when their cow came into her yard and ate many
of the flours she did not complain but helped Soni
catch the animal and tie it in a way that it could only
eat the grass.

They often sat for tea and special bread made only by the
Burusho.

Mel Gibson put out a movie about Jesus and someone sent Jon
and Jerri a copy. Later one Saturday afternoon they made cookies
and tea and invited the whole family over to watch the movie. It was
a long movie but quite interesting. They had a projector that played
the discs so they displayed the movie on a sheet stretched on the
wall. A few months earlier they already shared the gospel the best
they could and the family all agreed to trust Jesus. Their hope was
that the movie would help them understand more about His sacrifice
and His calling all of us into heaven after sacrificing His life to pay
our way and cleanse us from our sins.

Their reaction to the movie was not what they expected. They ate
the cookies while looking straight ahead and sipped their tea in the
same manner. It was near the end of the long movie that a response
was beginning to register. Like an earthquake which may start with
a little shaking they showed some response then more as time went
by and then all the women and girls were covering their faces with
their shalls. Ahamad's head was nodding down occasionally. At the
end, all the women and girls were bursting into tears, and Ahamad's
chin was on his chest. He was silent and still except for a jerk upwards
of his chin and emitting a sob that was quite sporadic. Jon and Jerri
were alarmed and were not sure what to do next.

The projector was off. A few minutes passed then Jon put his
hand on Ahamad's shoulder and he reached out to Jon and held on
to his arm and cried: "I am so sorry for Jesus. We can do nothing to
help." Not knowing what to do next Jon raised his voice a little and
addressed all in the room and said: "Jesus is alive now as we have seen
in the movie that He has risen. He wants us to be with Him always,
today and forever. Remember how we prayed together, and you asked

Jesus to come to you and save you? In that same way we will pray with you all today and ask Him for forgiveness of any sin we have and we join with Him now to overcome our sorrow with peace as He shows his love for us today. Jesus loves you."

The neighbours went back to their house next door after gaining some composure.

Many doors opened for us to share around town after this encounter and in general other people there were starting to trust us.

A few months later Jon and Jerri were called away to Kashmir and Ahamad wrote them this text: "Please come back to Gilgit we have neighbors, we need you."

Moving by Faith
to Kashmir

Following their time in Gilgit and Hispar, God called Jon and Jerri to Northern Kashmir, in India. Nothing seemed to have changed but the scenery. The people were much like the Burusho in northern Pakistan, but they were Kashmiri. Later Jon discovered that they were not far from the border.

Sometimes they were only seventy miles as the crow flies from their previous home in Gilgit.

Jon and Jerri loved the people and Kashmir. As far as winning the people it was about the same as Pakistan, maybe a little more difficult. Their goal of lighting the world on fire for the Lord was coming along about like rubbing two wet sticks together to start a fire. It was difficult for them and it seemed that time wasn't on their side.

As far as their living conditions and personal needs in general were not frustrating. Once they knew where to shop and how to travel.

Trip To Town For Supplies

One day a friend loaned me a vehicle so I could go into town for banking and supplies. I took Mansur, a local worker, with me. We found a parking place not far from the bank and parked the Jeep. I got out and headed toward the bank, while Mansur ran errands on the opposite side of the main street.

It was a hot July day. On the corner across the street were three soldiers with guns. They were on duty, watching the traffic and the pedestrians. One was a tall young man with a mustache that conspicuously underlined his prominent nose. He looked warm in his brown uniform.

The general store was just two stores down the street. There were ice cream treats in the store, and I thought of going there after the bank. I could get several treats, like the almond chocolate ones with vanilla ice cream and give them to the soldiers. Perhaps they would like to hear about Jesus. Even if they did not, it would be good to have them feel friendly toward me in case we interacted in the future.

I finished my banking and stepped out onto the sidewalk. Finding a safe place to cross the street, I turned toward the general store. Suddenly, I heard the sound of rapid gunfire and the whiz of bullets flying overhead! I froze, then dropped below the level of the cars, seeking shelter. The sound was coming from the street corner where the soldiers had been standing. I couldn't see them, but I had a nervous feeling about them.

After about a dozen shots, I heard a motorcycle racing away at top speed. The street fell silent. All the pedestrians had fled the scene. Still crouching behind cars, I called out for Mansur. When I looked up and saw someone was walking toward the intersection. I started to move forward to where I could see between the parked cars.

There in the middle of the street lay the tall young man with the mustache. His hands and arms were straight beside him and one leg was curled back under him. Two distinct holes went through his uniform into the middle of his chest. Two fountains of blood were streaming from the holes, squirting upward a few inches in time with his beating heart. The other soldiers were trying to help.

I began looking for Mansur and found him at the Jeep. We went directly back to my apartment.

The event made us heartsick. More than ever we longed for an effective way to share life with these people.

In a short while Jon and Jerri would have to pass a review by their overseers. The meeting would happen in another country. It would have a lot to do with their future. Pressure was on, and they were praying for a breakthrough. Conflicts that kept them from their goal of starting something credible were having a fierce impact on them personally. Every turn seemed to take them into a blind alley.

Stringent rules needed for security were part of it. Jon started going to the local Mosque for weekly prayers and wearing the locally accepted clothing to do so. Their friends in the area were uncomfortable with this so he stopped. This adversely effected their Islamic friends who could not imagine a good reason for not dressing properly if you could.

On the flip side anything not showing attendance to local dress could draw local attention. The crusades were long ago, but it seems the reaction is still in effect. Every child is expected to memorise their Holy book. Some accomplish this by the age of four. The reason for this is for them to know what is acceptable and what to reject. It is a safety issue for them. There seemed to be no middle ground for either side concerning religious bias and volumes of conflict to be had with little effort.

Just a few days before Jon and Jerri were to go for a check up on their progress and counseling, Jon was in Srinagar, on the edge of Dahl Lake for a bit of lunch at a lakeside restaurant. It was under shade trees with a spacious walkway framed and fit on posts anchored out onto Dahl Lake like a dock. He sat down and was waited on quickly by a young man named Joseph. He smiled at Jon and took his order and busily swept several honeybees from the table. Jon ordered rice and dahl with tea. The waiter came to the table later and asked where Jon was from? He said California and the man's eyes opened wide: "You are from California?" Jon tried to change the subject by asking if he was interested in God. To this he said: "Of course." Then, Jon went right into sharing: "Steps to Peace with God. By Billy Grahm." Joseph responded with a spark of interest. Unfortunately, his boss signaled him to bus another table. He did this quickly and looked quite smart at achieving it. Jon thought this guy is really a bright individual and interested in the truth. He could turn out to help us do something credible. Joseph balanced the food on a tray and smartly approached the table and placed the food and drink thereon. Jon began to eat quickly as the bees were visiting. The lunch was ok, but his mind was on winning this person.

Jon finished eating and the waiter cleared the table. With a smile he said that he now has a break and can talk more for a few minutes. They decided to walk out on the dock to the open water of the lake so they could talk more personally. Jon shared: "The wages of sin is death, but the gift of God is eternal life.' Are you interested to trust God to forgive you of your sins and give you eternal life?" Joseph replied: "I will have to think about that." He asked: "How are things in California?"

They talked a bit more, and too soon he stated: "Now I have to get back to work. Come back again and tell me more." Jon waved goodbye to Joseph and turned to go.

On the left side of the boardwalk was a clothing shop. Jon stepped in and tried to get a dialog going with a burly frizzy faced guy. It was of no avail as the person was a non-English speaker and his mind was shut like a trap door. He refused to listen about anything but the local religon. Jon remembered how open the waiter was and thanked the Lord! On the way home it appeared two teenagers were being detained by the security force. Possibly they were taken in for questioning as they were shuffled into the back of a grey colored police vehicle with no back windows. It was alarming and a cause for prayer and more reason to quickly get back to the apartment.

Two days later Jon went back to the restaurant, but it was vacant with no one in sight. He went over to the clothing shop and called out a greeting. The frizzy store clerk came to the door and Jon asked why is the restaurant closed? Frizzy looked at him and in a serious way and related best he could that the young man helping at the restaurant there had died yesterday. He said: "He fell into the lake right there and drowned." Jon had a lump in his throat and could not reply. He walked out on the dock and stared down at the water and began to cry. All the way back to the apartment he looked up to heaven and asked: "Please be with Joseph's family, and please help us overcome this!"

As they were packing for the trip abroad they mused about their position and of whether they would get to stay.

They could have claimed some success as there were some locals who came to the Lord and began a trust relationship with them. However, there were none that were willing to share the good news with their neighbors or to gather to worship and pray.

SEEKING GOOD COUNSEL

The next day they gathered in another country to consider the Lord's direction according to reports from the field and the experiences in reaching out to people in the area where they served. A report was given by those who were responsible for them, and Jon and Jerri had an opportunity to give their report. Their counselors listened carefully and pondered things according to the incoming facts. Good advice would be welcome and God advice precious. Jon and Jerri were praying they could stay.

It was quite a time of listening to their counselors. All this was aimed at what would be their next step in serving the Lord.

Jon told the story about meeting with Joseph on the shore of Dahl Lake. The overseers lamented with Jon and Jerri over the story of Joseph.

A few minutes went by then Jon told another story that could reveal a better picture with a positive influence they were having in the area. It was about something that happened several months before at their apartment in Srinagar.

This is the story:

The ground floor apartment was for the caretaker of the apartments. Sami was a pleasant young fellow and did well at keeping up the flower beds and the clipped grass in the enclosure. Jon had witnessed the gospel to Sami and his cousin. They were the ones who invited him to the mosque.

They both said yes to Jesus in prayer and accepted Him as their savior. It was difficult for them to understand many of the things shared about Christ, but they did not oppose hearing about Him.

It was not fully springtime and some of the nights were still quite cold. Jon had brought down a treat for Sami and his cousin who was staying the night. They opened their door and asked him to enter. The room was like a bedroom with chairs and a table. A small radio and two plates were on the table and a small bible he had given them.

In Kashmir on cold nights, it is common for family and company to sit in a room together after supper with one very long wool blanket that stretches around the room covering every person. All would sit and visit for the evening, and some would even sleep there for the night. If it was really cold, they would pass a kangri with burning charcoal inside, around and under the blanket to warm each person.

The boys were on the bed with a wool blanket for warmth and pillows to recline on. They asked Jon if he would read the bible to them. He said yes and they invited him onto the bed between them so they could hear the words. They reclined together with the blanket and below a single bulb of light. Jon began to read the 15th chapter of the Book of John. He squinted to read the small letters on the little bible. Far into the chapter the cousin spoke out a question: "Uncle Jon. We are disciples, right?"

He answered back: "Yes, you are surely His disciples." A little later he looked down at the two boys and they were sound asleep. He carefully crawled out from under the blanket and stretched it back over the boys and went back upstairs for the night.

The overseers liked the story and Jon could see a tear on Jerri's cheek. It spoke to him about her commitment to keep following the Lord in Kashmir.

The conclusion of their counsel was good, and simple. Yes, they should return to Kashmir, but possibly to another area.

They packed up their things and proceeded back to India and later to Kashmir.

DESPERATION AND BREAKTHROUGH!

BREAKTHROUGH WITH A SHORT STORY

They returned to India and stopped for a few days in New Delhi to break before returning to Kashmir. There was a special price for four days in a good hotel and they decided to stop and spend time praying and asking God to show them what He wanted them to do concerning their call to Kashmir.

They spent four days of fasting and praying and listening to the Lord as they read the scriptures. It was the fourth night and after 10;00 PM. Jon turned out the lights and told his wife goodnight and went back into the living room. In Jon's words: "We knew the Lord was with us and calling us to win souls and pray for laborers for the harvest. When speaking to Zacchaeus Jesus said in Luke 19:10: "for the Son of Man has come to seek and to save that which was lost." Then He said later according to John 20:21: "So Jesus said to them again, "Peace to you! As the Father has sent Me, I also send you." From this and other parts of the bible they knew His calling is sure for them to seek and to save lost souls.

The following is from Jon:

One lamp was on the table and my bible with a notebook of writing papers that were beside it. I sat and looked straight ahead. I asked: What shall we do? What shall we do to win all You want us to win? I opened the bible and opened the notebook and picked up a pencil and held it over the notebook. I said again, Lord what shall we do? I was fading but tried to think.

Then something came to me about the biggest problem we faced. We had a huge problem with everything we presented about God to most of the local people it was turning from discussion into an argument. When I asked Him how to stop arguing the very next thought was, write a story. What story? It immediately came to me to write a story from John chapter three and make it about Jesus. I started and it came clear and fast. Though I have studied this many times I never spent much time on verses John 3:14 & 15. This time it took my attention and became a major part of the story. We needed a powerful invitation that is sensible to all people. What could be better than one based on a yes or no answer to a question about an opportunity to be saved like the people with Moses did when they chose to obey after their horrible actions then look up to receive one of the greatest second chances in history? What would we do if we were there and were bitten, wouldn't we say yes to God and look upon the serpent on the pole as Moses instructed, or would we just die?

It is classic and designed by the Lord. Not perishing is a huge plus for anyone in a life and death situation, and according to the scriptures every person on earth is in that situation until they have Jesus Christ. Romans 3:23: "for all have sinned and fall short of the glory of God." Then Romans 6:23: "For the wages of sin is death, but the gift of God is eternal life in Christ Jesus our Lord."

Right close to 4:30 AM I was finished with the story. It was still a little rough, but I was confident to tell it. We called it the Lifestory on August 8, 2009.

Jerri stirred from my noise, and I told her, "We don't need to worry anymore about where we are going to serve the Lord nor how we are going to serve Him." She accepted this news quietly and drifted off back to sleep. I was primed because I had the story.

I told her I was planning to visit the kitchen around 7:00 before it opened, to see if I could find anyone to tell the

story to. I spent the next two hours imagining what it would be like to tell it to someone.

Seven o'clock finally rolled around, and with a mixtureof curiosity, trepidation, faith, and excitement I headed downstairs. Sure enough, the chef was available. He appeared to possibly be Islamic. He was also quite tall and a good English speaker. It was easy to tell him the story, although he had to lean over the counter to lend me his prominent ears. Except for a brief interruption to direct one of the cooks, he gave me his full attention.

I never imagined the result! All my previous efforts to present the Gospel with apologetics had provoked endless objections and they could never hold a candle to what just happened.

The chef gave a clear and firm yes to trusting Jesus without raising a single argument. And he thanked me profusely.

LIFESTORY ANSWER TO OUR PRAYERS

Back in their room, Jon told Jerri about his experience. She was amazed, yet not quite sure what to think. Finally, he was able to sleep. At about 11:00 a.m., there was a knock on our door. Two young men were there. Both had dark faces and short beards. They seemed to have an important message for us. Jon and Jerri listened carefully and deciphered their broken English. They were told: That Jon was to come down to the lobby at 11:00 PM. The chef will have some people for me to meet with and to tell the same story that was told to him. Jon said: "Oh, of course. I will be there at 11:00 PM."

Jon felt nervous yet tired from the previous night. Jerri was not surprised that he slept much of the day. He spent the rest of the day reviewing the Lifestory in case there would be a barrage of questions.

When evening came, he was alert with anticipation. After all, they had heard from Jesus, and the Lifestory was a success so far. They prayed that appropriate answers would come to mind if there was an inquisition. They also prayed for the grace not to argue about anything.

Just before 11:00 p.m., Jon opened the door and started down the dark hall to the spiral staircase. Only a few people were still in the restaurant downstairs. The area was lush and green, with a fountain nestled among the foliage. A long table was placed off to one side, and a counter stretched right to the kitchen door.

Some workers were busy mopping, and others were arranging chairs. When Jon reached the landing at the bottom of the stairs, one of the waiters came and ushered him to a seat at one of the tables. At least *he* seemed to know what was happening. Though the chef was not in sight.

Jon looked up as a man named Tarik came and sat across from him at the table. His notably dark hair was well trimmed but long enough to lie back on top. He gently explained that he spoke English and asked if Jon would please tell him the same story he had told the chef that morning.'

Jon's first words came out a little less dignified, as his throat became tensed. He felt cautious, with

questions like, *Why isn't the chef here? Is this a kind of Asian CIA thing?* Jon did not stare at him, but kept a conscious track of his reactions to each part of the story.

After hearing the Lifestory, Tarik came to Jesus in nearly the same way as the chef had. He gave a clear yes and prayed for the Lord to come into his life and save him. With tears, he asked if God would forgive Him for something he had done. Jon was a bit shocked, but assured him

that God would forgive him if he would admit to the Lord that what he had done was wrong and then ask Jesus Christ for forgiveness. He listened to I John 1:9: "If we confess our sins, He is faithful and just to forgive us our sins and to cleanse us form all unrighteousness." He then confessed his sins and prayed for the Lord's forgiveness.

After their conversation, he got up and moved aside but stayed close enough to be a translator for the others who were coming. Jon was most thankful for his help.

Ayjaz came and sat across from me. He worked as a shift manager. Much of his black hair was escaping his white cap. Since he was not as fluent in English so Tarik helped with the language difference. He also sacrificed to stay late to interpret and make sure they all heard the Lifestory.

And so it went. One by one, each came and sat across from Jon and asked to hear the Lifestory. After they heard it, each one prayed and promised to follow Jesus. Everyone who heard the story expressed both relief and gratitude.

Some asked for prayer for various issues. Others asked, "What can I do about the wrong I have done?"

"You have already been forgiven by trusting in Jesus," Jon answered. "Remember the serpent on the pole? That is God's sign that your debt has been paid in full." He then went on to explain, "God loves you, and Jesus has paid for you. You have done the right thing by turning away from sin and accepting the truth that you need Jesus to take away your debt and make you clean. You are now free from eternal death.

We have to live a clean life so we confess the sins we know of and He promises forgiveness in I John 1:9, which reads: "If we confess our sins, He is faithful and just to forgive us our sins & cleanse us from all unrighteousness."

"We must always be grateful to God because it cost Him the blood and death of His Son, He was incarnated as a man to pay that price to save us. Now we trust in Jesus, not ourselves, because He overcame death for us."

This is reassured according to 2 Corinthians 5:21, which reads: "For He made Him who knew no sin to be sin for us, that we might become the righteousness of God in Him."

By the end of the evening, Jon had told each person the Lifestory and prayed with them individually. A few had already left for their homes, but others stayed to thank him again. He shook their hands and hugged them. Amazingly, the whole event only took a little over two hours.

Nine heard the Lifestory that night. All nine declared their desire to trust Jesus and receive salvation. In all our interaction, there was no mention of religion.

Their modest work clothes and gentle manner were much like that of the chef Jon had met earlier that morning. Their response to the Lifestory now revealed the Spirit was encouraging like a kindred spirit between them and Jon as well.

Upon finally retiring to their hotel room, Jon told Jerri the exciting news. When she heard of the great things that had happened, she was elated. With hearts full of praise, they continually blessed the Lord that night for answering their prayers by giving them this Lifestory.

Receiving the Lifestory was a new beginning for them, and it solved two major concerns. First: How can they introduce all these people to Jesus? Answer: They had a solid, non-confrontational way to introduce everyone to Jesus! Second: Where to position themselves on the field? Answer: The positive reaction from different hearers who were from different locations seems to make the geographic limitations seem to be less of a problem.

It was becoming a reality that this story will take us into consultation with an open variety of prospects.

God was answering their prayers. They were hearing the voice of Jesus in their hearts from His word and were following Him. There was still a small question about how this Lifestory would work in other areas. It is time now to go and try it and find out themselves.

First Street Witnessing
with the Lifestory

The morning after the breakthrough in the hotel dining room, we left the hotel and ventured out into the street. Our first stop was a shop we thought might have an item we needed. The shopkeepers were two young men who looked to be twins. One asked what I was looking for.

"First, I have a short story. Would you like to hear it?" I replied.

"Yes, of course. Go ahead," they both agreed.

I proceeded to tell them the Lifestory. They listened so intently that I had to focus on staying on track. Why were they staring? I got to the part when we talk about the symbol of the serpent on the pole, and one of them blurted out, "Yes, we have seen this also."

This encouraging response eased my tension.

Jesus drew them into the Lifestory. When I asked them to decide whether to trust Jesus to also save them, they simultaneously replied, "Yes!" We then prayed with them for Jesus to come into their lives and save them. The shop came alive with their happy shouts, and Jerri joined them in shouting for joy.

We left the shop as new friends, with hugs and handshakes. Sharing the Lord with the twins gave Jerri and me a good feeling because we have twin sons. It is always a treat for us to meet twins. This was God's way of delivering us from the earlier frustration of fruitlessness. This victory was medicine for our hearts.

Crossing the avenue, we came upon some children. They spoke only their local language, but a smile is universal. We snapped a picture to remind us to ask Jesus, "What can we do for these dear ones? How can we introduce them to you?"

The answer came as we began to see the Lord loving children through their parents and other loved ones. Seeing their ramshackle house, we guessed that these kids were from a poor family. They may have been orphans.

We talked with them the best we could with the language we had acquired, but we did not get very far with the Lifestory. It was easy to love them, so we tried to bless them with affection and encouragement. They grinned and tried to follow us for a short distance.

Jerri and I held hands as we walked away. We lifted our eyes and prayed for them as we sang, "Jesus loves the little children. Including all the children of the world." We prayed that someday we would bring laborers to service the little people and the children.

WARRIOR WAITERS

Later that day we acted as tourists, following a recommendation for a Chinese restaurant near the zoo in Delhi. The taxi driver was a friendly man named Ahmed. He was from the Indian state of Bihar. The road was paved but narrow. We reached the restaurant and found it nestled in a clump of trees. Our driver waited for us in the parking lot. We brought him some food later.

The attractive building was one story, with interior and floors made of hardwood, and the walls were highly decorated. It looked pricy for our budget, but we went inside anyway. A smartly dressed waiter quickly appeared. He had strong East Asian features and a robust physique. His English was excellent. He introduced himself as Natal.

The first thing I asked was, "I have a short story. Would you like to hear it?"

He answered, "I will come back with some water, then you can tell me. But it has to be short."

"That is good," I agreed.

When he returned, I quickly related the Lifestory, trying not to draw the attention of the other patrons or staff.

At the end of the Lifestory, I asked if he would look up to Jesus and trust Him to save him also.

"Yes," he clearly stated. He strode back to the kitchen and returned with menus. He told me his brother also worked there and asked if I would tell him the story too.

After lunch, we walked out on the porch and waited until they joined us. Much like Natal, his brother came to Jesus immediately. While they visited with us later, they told me they were from the mountains of Nepal, and they were warriors in their home area. I said to them:

"Now you are warriors for Jesus," As we said goodbye for the last time all of us agreed that we hoped to see each other again someday.

I could detect very little difference between the way these Buddhist men came to Jesus through the Lifestory and how the Muslim men we had met earlier came to Jesus.

MANAGED BY THE MANAGER

Ahmed, our kind taxi driver, drove us to the hotel.

A messenger greeted us at the door. "The manager would like to speak with you."

Gulping, I replied, "Sure. I'll be right down as soon as I take my wife to our room."

I felt apprehensive, so I said a short prayer before returning to the front desk. I relaxed when I was greeted by two smiling ladies. I told them the manager had requested to see me. One of them directed me to the door of his office.

Looking through the glass door, I tapped lightly to get his attention. He was sitting at his desk and signaled for me to enter. I noticed he was well dressed and seemed rather self-disciplined. We exchanged greetings, then I asked how I could be of help.

"You are telling things to our workers. I would like to know: Are you a preacher?"

"No, I am a retired person, but I often tell people a short story. Would you like to hear it?"

"You know, I might as well. It seems everyone else has heard it! Go ahead. Tell me the story."

I started telling the Lifestory and got to the part where it explains that even today, in this city, there is a symbol of a serpent on a pole on some medical facilities.

Then I asked, "If you were with me in front of Moses, wouldn't we both have looked up to the serpent on the pole rather than die of a terrible serpent bite?"

He stalled, then said, "I suppose so, but this is just a story, right?"

I saw he was tense and defensive, and I remembered how I felt years before when a preacher asked if I knew I was a sinner. I hoped with all my heart the preacher wouldn't ask me to name all the bad things I had done. Thanks be to God, he did not.

The manager was clearly anxious. Watching carefully for any sign of the Holy Spirit at work, I continued with the Lifestory.

In situations like this, Jerri and I realized that we, together with God, are coming alongside a person who may be facing the living God for the first time. We think it is good for everyone to have someone journey with them through this experience. And we don't want any argument to derail the Lifestory. If a question comes up, we say, "That's a good question. Could we hold that until after the story, then try to answer it?" So that's what I told the manager.

I reached the last part of the Lifestory. "Now, my friend," I said, "I know Jesus loves you, and He is drawing you to himself right now. He doesn't want you to perish because of your sins and mistakes. He wants you to have eternal life with Him. So I have one question for you. Remember how the terrible serpents bit the people? They looked up to the serpent on the pole, and they were saved. In the same way, Jesus is inviting you to look up to Him right now so He can also save you. So my question is simple; Yes or no?"

He paused, and I waited quietly for his decision. It is best to let the Holy Spirit do the talking from here on. I was sure he would answer when he was ready.

"Not right now," he said. "I have a lot to do for now. Thank you for sharing your story."

I think God was touching his heart, but he clearly wanted to stop there. I got up, thanked him for seeing me, and wished him good evening. It felt a little sad, but I thanked the Lord as I went up to the room. I told Jerri what had happened. We agreed that his decision must be accepted and respected.

Fare To Heaven Paid

Ahmed, our taxi driver, was the next person to hear the Lifestory. It was easy to see he was very poor. One of the rubber loops on his right sandal was broken and crudely mended with an old piece of fabric. He was young and by his slight beard, we thought him to be about twenty.

As I paid the fare and said goodbye for the day, I asked if he had five minutes to hear a short story.

"Yes sir," he replied.

I told the Lifestory, and he accepted the invitation to ask for forgiveness of sin and for the Lord Jesus to save his soul. As we prayed together, I considered that his worn out clothes and old shoes meant nothing compared to the great value of his tender heart and the riches of grace that Jesus freely adorned him with that day.

His prayer for the Lord's forgiveness for his sin was sincere. He said, "Forgive me and come into my heart now and save me. I will follow Jesus." Then he asked me, "Sir, will you come with me to Bihar? We need you in Bihar."

I did not respond but pondered his request in my heart for some time.

It was good that his taxi was near our hotel because we needed his services quite often over the next three days.

DAVID IN THE DEN

The next person we told the Lifestory to was David, who we met at the Hard Rock Cafe. Some may ask us why we chose such a loud place. For one thing, it had been recommended to us as a good place for American food. It was also a venture into the unknown for us, and thus a challenge.

We reached the café through a large shopping mall. The directions we were given said it would be downstairs at the west end of the mall, behind a set of imposing wooden doors. Sure enough, the doors were there. We entered and were directed to a table.

Once inside, we realized we needed a table where the music wasn't so loud. They led us to an adjoining room, where it was blissfully quiet.

After glancing at the prices, we decided to get just one sandwich and split it. Fortunately, the sandwich was big enough for both of us.

A young waiter came to take our order. I asked if the door to the other room could be shut a little further so I could hear his questions. I got the impression he was new to the work and a little homesick. Carefully and respectfully, he addressed me as Father. We were touched by his excellent British accent. Everything he said was impressive to us. After a few minutes, he said, "My home in Nepal is too far to visit. I have not seen my parents in two years, and my name is David."

We agreed that his feelings were certainly normal, and we felt sympathy for him. Jerri told him our names and returned a comment about how we, too, were missing our home in the United States. The conversation was kept as short as possible because of his attention to his work responsibilities.

David brought us both a glass of ice water and took our order back into the kitchen area. Jerri and I talked and observed some of the pictures on the wall, then David came back in and sat down beside me. Earlier I had mentioned a short story, and now he wanted to hear it. We were the only guests in that area, so it was a good setting for telling the Lifestory.

He listened with interest and answered yes to my question about looking up to the serpent.

Next came the corresponding passage in which Jesus said, "And I, if I am lifted up from the earth, will draw all peoples to Myself" (John 12:32).

My next words went like this: "Since you have said yes, God will give you the way to pray a short prayer with me. Is that okay with you?" He said: "Yes,"

I invited him to follow me in prayer. He followed and said, "I, David, ask Jesus Christ to forgive my sin and come into my life. I will follow Jesus. Amen."

We talked a little more about following, and I made sure he knew a way to follow Jesus by reading the scripture every day. In his situation, it was best that he download a Bible app. It was good, and he liked the idea of starting with the book of John.

WHO'S AT THE ZOO?

Our next excursion was to the Delhi Zoo. It was 8:00 a.m. when we arrived, but the gate didn't open until 8:30 a.m. At first the gatekeeper insisted on waiting until the exact time; then he changed his mind. He gave us our tickets early, before the rest of the people. My wife had suggested I ask for this. I felt a little sheepish, but I asked, and it happened.

We were scheduled to travel later that day, so we went rather quickly through the zoo, arriving back at the front gate just as the zoo opened its gates. As is common in India, a mass of people came rushing in. I stood amazed as I asked the Lord, "Which one shall I share with?"

In my heart, I heard Him answer, "All of them."

"Shall I find an apple box and stand before this crowd and begin to tell the Lifestory?"

God was silent. Later He answered my question through a personal experience that taught me to leave out no one.

Reaching the outside of the gate, I asked the gatekeeper, "Would you like to hear a short story? It will take about five minutes."

He answered: "Yes, sahib."

I told him the Lifestory, and he came to Jesus. I gently touched the top of his white cotton garment as he prayed for Jesus to come into his life and save him.

Immediately after the prayer, he asked, "How can I learn more about Jesus?"

"I am glad you asked me this question. I have recently purchased a Hindi Bible. Can you read Hindi?" I asked.

"Yes," he said. I directly went to the cab, retrieved the Bible, and brought it to the grateful Indian. As we drove away, I could see him studying it.

GONE TO GOA

By this time, Jerri and I were so excited about the Lifestory that we were dreaming of new ways we could use it. The experience at the hotel had been so encouraging that we considered that God was leading us to specifically share in hotels. After all, we had only stayed at this one hotel for four days, and the fruit was forty souls. Even possibly one more if the manager came to Jesus after we left him.

We saw an ad for a special weeklong tourist trip to Goa and decided to sign up, with the idea that we could tell the Lifestory four times a day while seeing the sights. Off to the airport we went to catch the plane to Goa.

That's when I made a serious blunder, or so it seemed. I left our camera in the airport security. It wasn't until we were in the air that I noticed it was missing. The camera loss bothered me. I wanted to blame it on the devil, but God used it for the salvation of many.

The first to be saved was a nice lady working in the Goa Airport. Her name was Shoni, and she came to Jesus without hesitation. Her father was Buddhist, but they were already looking for Jesus.

She did everything she could to find our camera and get it to Goa so we could take pictures of all the wonderful sights there.

The best thing was her attitude; she was so industrious. Right away, Shoni contacted the airline to help with our problem. She sat down with us and wanted to hear more about Jesus. Everything we showed her in the Word about Him was such an amazement to her.

We told her where we were staying, and she said it was a nice place. She looked at us and said, "You have to come back here tomorrow at two. By then I will have news for you about your camera."

We agreed to come back and wished her God's blessing. She put us in a cab and sent us on our way.

It was late when we arrived at our hotel, but it didn't matter, because we were having so much fun leading the taximan to Jesus.

He was a needy soul. His wife had struggled with an illness for many years. The stress could be heard in his voice, especially when he talked about his kids. She had died nearly a year earlier, but he needed the healing touch of Jesus now. We shared the Lifestory, and he followed God's instructions about trusting in Jesus. We praised God for this victory for him, and we were thrilled to find out he was Shoni's uncle.

We continued to minister to him until we reached our hotel, helping him pray through the issues his family was dealing with. He was excited to hear about a way to confess sin and be cleansed of our failures in 1 John 1:9: "If we confess our sins, He is faithful and just to forgive us our sins and to cleanse us from all unrighteousness."

Next we met a man named Tim who was sure that we should move to Goa. He was a local real estate agent whose family owned a number of properties near the beach. He invited us to his house to meet his mother and enjoy a Goan dinner. I felt the dinner would be a good opportunity for Jerri and me to tell the Lifestory to them.

Tim picked us up from the hotel and took us on a narrow, winding road through the jungle. At first there were no houses, which made me nervous. The jungle fell back, and we drove through a large stone gate. Tim explained that this had been his home all his life.

With its tall, pointed roof, the house seemed typical of the architecture in the area. Tim guided us up the steps to the front door. Leaving our shoes outside, we entered. His mother came to greet us wearing a silk sari and a big smile.

The kitchen was one of the largest rooms in the house. We got to see it, but we did not go inside. I noticed that most of the cooking pans were quite large. The aroma was enough to help us overcome any hesitation about trying the local food. Tim's mother was very busy preparing the food, so she didn't join us in the living room. As we made ourselves comfortable, I noticed there were several fabric-covered chairs and a sofa, all apparently from the 1960s.

Tim told us of houses near the beach and showed us pictures and statistics about the value of each. In less than fifteen minutes, the food was on the dining room table, and we were called to be seated. I asked to pray and made it short and respectful in the name of Jesus Christ. I then mentioned I had a short story to tell them after dinner.

Dinner was delicious. After we finished, I started telling the Lifestory, but suddenly the house began to shake!

A terrible noise came from upstairs. It sounded like a bunch of madmen stomping on the floor. And it got even louder, like they were running full speed from one end of the house to the other.

My story had been cut short by a troop of monkeys, huge monkeys with a very belligerent attitude. Tim apologized for forgetting to close the attic so that they could not come in.

I told him the rest of the Lifestory in his car on the way back to the hotel. He seemed much more concerned that we had not signed a buyer's agreement and given him earnest money on one of the homes. I apologized to Tim for not telling him the Lifestory when we first met. This would have saved him making dinner for us.

"Are those monkeys dangerous?" I asked.

"We allow them to do their way."

From his answer, I supposed he might be a Hindu.

Our short time in Goa was exhilarating. We enjoyed it so much that we wanted to stay longer, but we couldn't due to other responsibilities back in Kashmir.

Sharpening the Lifestory

We left Goa after introducing many in the hotel and on the beach to Jesus. At one point people followed us along the road, asked if we were church leaders, and brought us gifts. Several asked us to stay. We thought about it, prayed, but our commitment was to Kashmir.

On our way home, more souls came to Jesus. First was the lady at the airport information window in the international airport in Delhi, who told me how to find the lost and found department. She had time to hear the story and pray to receive the Lord. When I arrived at the lost and found, five more people heard the Lifestory and gave their lives to Jesus.

Back in Kashmir, we began telling the Lifestory. Our experiences over the next year and a half could fill volumes. It became evident that Lifestory movements were to be a major part of our future.

While it is very easy to tell the Lifestory, it is also very easy *not* to tell it. We quickly came up with a strategy to overcome any reluctance on our part. We made a commitment to the Lord to tell the Lifestory four times a day for one month. It was simple, yet it still felt like an adventure. We would have to give up some personal time and change our attitude about interacting with everyday people.

For example, going to the store would now include buying bread, toothpaste, fruit, and taking five minutes to tell someone the Lifestory.

Easy, right? Not so fast! Would the owner be annoyed if we interrupted someone else's shopping?

We prayed and decided to try speaking to the owner or manager first. That approach turned out well.

Usually the owner or manager wanted to hear the Lifestory. They often said yes to Jesus and prayed with us. Sometimes they would gather the staff so they could also hear the Lifestory. Occasionally, they would say, "No, do not tell it in the store." We accepted all this as we continued to praise the Lord and share the Lifestory. Each interaction taught us more. As the Gospel that had been bound in our hearts was released into the world, abundant life began to flow.

We found that questions were invaluable. We asked people if they would look up and trust Jesus to save them in the same way the people following Moses were saved when they looked up to the serpent on the pole. This required a yes or no answer. Many said yes and then prayed to receive Jesus when invited to do so in the same way.

Sometimes the person we spoke with would be silent for a few moments, then tears would stream down their cheeks. We should always try to be sensitive to the Lord and give people the time they need to hear and respond to Jesus without interrupting them.

After someone said yes, we would invite them to pray a simple, short prayer: "My name is _____. I invite Jesus into my life. I will follow Jesus."

We would also ask, "What did you like best about the story?"

On a few occasions, we heard responses so filled with profound wisdom that they must have come from the mind of the Lord. One Muslim cleric at a *masjid* in Srinagar answered, "I like the part where Jesus tells us when we are born again we are eternal."

I asked him which part of the story this was in?

He replied, "You know, where Jesus says we are like the wind. It has no beginning, and it has no end, and we are just like that, eternal."

What a great response from someone who was only minutes old in the Lord, especially as he came from a people who have little knowledge of Jesus!

At the end of the Lifestory, after someone receives Jesus, we ask a question that encourages them to follow the Lord even more closely: "Can you think of someone who would also appreciate this story?"

If they say yes, the next question is, "Could you see yourself being the person to tell them this story if it was quick and enjoyable for you to learn?" If they answer yes to this question, we tell them when and where the training will be available.

JON SMITH

LIFESTORY WITH SCRIPTURES

Instructions: To be prepared to tell it now. Use the tellable copy. It is more of a paraphrase and is short and more effective in winning people quickly and helpful when teaching it to others rapidly. We will post a tellable copy in an addendum. In this part, you may enjoy finding the scriptures related to the Lifestory.

It starts:

I have a short story. It takes five minutes. Would you like to hear it?

Wait for a "yes." If they pause or ask what it is about? you may say something like this: "OK, it is a story about the greatest second chance ever."

Great!

It is 2021. Most people know that, but not many people know why. The reason it is 2021 is simple: Time was stopped over two thousand years ago, and then it started again and carried on until this day. The important question: Why did time stop?

The reason time stopped is because God was looking into the status of every person, and He found that everyone was broken. No one can enter heaven if they are broken because of sin.

God sees the heart, according to 1 Samuel 16:7: "But the Lord said to Samuel, 'Do not look at his appearance or at his physical stature, because I have refused him. For the Lord does not see as man sees; for man looks at the outward appearance, but the Lord looks at the heart.'"

They are all broken, and no one can enter heaven when broken. Here is further proof of this brokenness in Romans 3:10: "As it is written: 'There is none righteous, no, not one.'" So, God came to earth and He fixed our problem. It is a new time, and the saviour is now here, according to Luke 2:11: "For there is born to you this day in the city of David a Saviour who is Christ the Lord."

God came down to earth and took on the form of a human and was born into the world like all of us. We can see this in John 1:14: "And the Word became flesh and dwelt among us, and we beheld His glory, the glory as of the only begotten of the Father, full of grace and truth."

He was here on earth, and He healed people, according to John 5:8: "Jesus said to him, 'Rise, and take up your bed and walk. And immediately the man was made well, took up his bed, and walked.'"

He even raised the dead, according to John 11:43,44: "Now when He had said these things, He cried with a loud voice, 'Lazarus, come forth!' And he who had died came out bound with graveclothes ...'"

The most important thing He did was to fix our problem of brokenness and sin, as stated in II Corinthians 5:21: "For He made Him who knew no sin to be sin for us, that we might become the righteousness of God in Him."

He did this by living a perfect life, then gathered all the mistakes of every person and put them alongside His perfect life. With His great love, He exchanged his perfect life for our broken lives, took all our sin with Him down to the grave, and paid for it with His own blood, according to Revelations1:5: "And from Jesus Christ, the faithful witness, the firstborn from the dead, and the ruler over the kings of the earth. To Him who loved us and washed us from our sins in His own blood."

After that, He overcame death and went up into heaven, according to 1 Timothy 3:16: "And without controversy great is the mystery of godliness: God was manifested in the flesh, justified in the Spirit, seen by angels, preached among the Gentiles, believed on in the world, received up in glory."

The door is now open, so everyone who believes in Him and follows Him can come inside. This is revealed in 2 Corinthians 5:8: "We are confident, yes, well pleased rather to be absent from the body and to be present with the Lord." The only problem is, not many are going through this door, according to Matthew 7:14: "Because narrow is the gate and difficult is the way which leads to life, and there are few who find it." That's why I tell this story.

When God first made the world, there were no people in it, so He made two, Adam and Eve. They were very happy. And they were so close to God, like two clasped hands.

There was just one rule, according to Genesis 2:17: "But of the tree of the knowledge of good and evil you shall not eat, for in the day that you eat of it you shall surely die." But they ate from the tree and broke the rule. And they didn't just break the rule; they broke the relationship. It has been broken ever since that day. And now death reigns.

According to the book of Exodus and Numbers, this occurred about twenty five hundred years after Adam and Eve. God called a man named Moses to lead God's people out of Egypt, as revealed in Exodus 3:10: "Come now, therefore, and I will send you to Pharaoh that you may bring My people, the children of Israel, out of Egypt." Moses was to lead more than a million people from Egypt to the promised land. During this journey, the people did evil in the sight of God, so God struck them with fiery serpents, and many of them died. Some ran to Moses and cried out, according to Numbers 21:7: "Therefore the people came to Moses, and said, 'We have sinned, for we have spoken against the Lord and against you; pray to the Lord that He take away the serpents from us.' So Moses prayed for the people."

Moses prayed, and God heard his prayer. God told Moses what to do, according to Numbers 21:8,9: "Then the Lord said to Moses, 'Make a fiery serpent, and set it on a pole, and it shall be that everyone who is bitten, when he looks at it, shall live." So Moses made a bronze serpent, and put it on a pole; and so it was, if a serpent had bitten anyone, when he looked at the bronze serpent, he lived."

Even today, in this city and in every city in the world, one might find this symbol in a hospital, on an ambulance, or in a pharmacy.

It is likely that you and I both would have looked up to the pole and serpent rather than die, wouldn't we? Thank you for saying yes, because this has something to do with the end of the story.

About fifteen hundred years after Moses, according to the ancient scriptures in the book of John in the New Testament of the Bible, this is what happened: It was a dark night, and there was a man in the street. His name was Nicodemus, and he was a great teacher of the law. He was looking for Jesus. When he found Jesus, Nicodemus said the following, according to John 3:2–4:

"This man came to Jesus by night and said to Him, "Rabbi, we know that You are a teacher come from God; for no one can do these signs that You do unless God is with him."

Jesus answered and said to him, "Most assuredly, I say to you, unless one is born again, he cannot see the Kingdom of God."

In John 3:4: "Nicodemus said to Him "How can a man be born when he is old? Can he enter a second time into his mother's womb and be born?"

Then again in John 3:5&6: Jesus answered, "Most assuredly, I say to you, unless one is born of water and the Spirit, he cannot enter the Kingdom of God." That which is born of the flesh is flesh, and that which is born of the Spirit is spirit. Then later in John 3:7: & 8:"Do not marvel that I said to God. You must be born again. The wind blows where it wishes, and you hear the sound of it, but cannot tell where it comes from and where it goes. So is everyone who is born of the Spirit."

Nicodemus replied in John 3:9: "Nicodemus answered and said to Him, 'How can these things be?'"

Then in John 3:14 & 15: "And as Moses lifted up the serpent in the wilderness, even so must the Son of Man be lifted up, that whoever believes in Him should not perish but have eternal life."

Now, my friend, I know Jesus loves you. He doesn't want you to ever perish. He wants you to have eternal life.

My question for you is very simple: Remember the part in the story of how the people looked up to that serpent on the pole and were saved?

The listener now gets an opportunity to answer yes or no. Yes, that is good. In the very same way, Jesus is inviting you to look up to Him today and trust Him to save you also. My question is, "Yes or no?"

[Wait for their response.]

Great! Now that God has touched your life, would you say a short prayer with me?

[Wait for their response.]

Great. Just follow me, and say your name where I indicate:

"Dear God, my name is _____.
I ask Jesus forgive my sins and to come into my life.
I will follow Jesus. Amen".

＊ ＊ ＊ ＊ ＊

For immediate next steps after someone trusts Jesus in response to the Lifestory please see the complete usable introduction and instructions to the five minute Lifestory in the appendix.

Timing and More Sharpening

There is a unanimous agreement among those who frequently tell the Lifestory that it should come before presenting other stories and ideas. This serves the Holy Spirit's desire to lead the lost to the savior, Jesus Christ, who is the truth.

The greatest moment in a Lifestory movement is when the Lifestory becomes the property of the people in a new language and culture. This is when we are obedient to pray and raise up laborers for the harvest. We must offer the Lifestory with respect and love. We don't get to choose who will respond. God draws certain souls into His family, respecting their own free will. Many are called, and few are chosen.

As Lifestory tellers, our aim is to give each person every encouragement to say yes to Jesus while making every effort to ensure the decision is truly theirs. We are coming alongside them to face the living God and for them it may be the first time. We aren't high-pressure salespeople. Rather, we are fishers seeking to catch whoever the Lord provides.

Being added to our spiritual family is the same for everyone, just as it is stated in Acts 2:47: "And the Lord added to the church daily those who were being saved." We are simply servants; only God can give the increase. Hearing from God through His word takes us into fruitful practices.

The timing of the Lifestory is important. The presentation must be short and to the point in order to be effective, as most people have short attention spans. In the early days, the Lifestory was too long, and we had to shorten it. God allowed us to see this clearly through Irfan.

Irfan was an easygoing young Muslim man and a college graduate. He had dark black eyebrows and hair to match.

We were living in Kashmir. Irfan joined me for a conference for relief workers in Delhi. It was my first train ride in India. At the station, we checked for the correct platform to wait for our train. I was glad we were early because I had never seen anything quite like this.

I intended to tell Irfan the Lifestory when we reached our platform. To get there, we had to climb some stairs that went up and over the tracks. We could see the trains coming and going below, and the platforms shook a little. The overpass was a good place to tell him the Lifestory because there were fewer people up there and a lot less noise.

As we walked, I asked him if he would like me to tell him a story. He agreed, so I began. It was a longer and wordier version than what we use now, but I got through it, and he said yes to the invitation to trust Jesus to save him. Now it was time for a prayer of commitment, but we were interrupted by the announcement that our train was arriving at platform three.

JON SMITH

Suddenly it seemed like a thousand people were rushing past us, many with their luggage on their heads. We managed to complete the prayer together, then hurried along to find the railcar assigned to us.

Unfortunately, the top bunk in the two-tiered car was near the air conditioner, and I had a cold. I was congested and had trouble breathing during the night.

The twelve-hour trip to Delhi took place at night, so we were unable to enjoy the scenery. Instead, I only got a glimpse of the streetlights flashing past and an occasional station. Every so often, a whoosh of air and the blast of the whistle announced the presence of a train speeding by us on the opposite track.

Even though I felt ill from the motion and the constant blast of cold air from the AC, I told the Lifestory to several other passengers in our railcar. I thought it would be good for Irfan to experience how others responded to the Lifestory. Perhaps it would also give him the idea that he, too, could tell the Lifestory.

My intentions and accomplishments are often two separate things. It is a good thing my best friend Jesus always accomplishes His intentions! I knew He would someday bring Irfan to be a Lifestory teller.

The train was slowing, and low buildings appeared on both sides of the track. More and more train tracks came into view. Here and there other trains were standing quietly. We were coming into Delhi. I still didn't feel very well, and I was happy the train ride was over. It seemed better things were close at hand, like a bath and a good sleep.

The train came to a stop in Delhi. There was mass confusion as everyone got off. Once outside the station, we encountered a multitude of three-wheeled taxis lining the roadways, seeking passengers.

We climbed into one, and Irfan directed the driver to our destination. Upon reaching the hotel, we produced our passports and proceeded to check in. I asked the three men at the front desk if they would like to hear a short story. They said yes.

No other customers were there at the time, which made it even easier, so I told them the Lifestory.

They told God they were inviting Jesus into their lives and would follow Him. Moments later, as we were heading up the stairs to our room, I asked Irfan for his opinion on how well I was telling the Lifestory. He replied, "It is boring."

I then asked, "Is that because you have heard it quite a few times?"

"No," he insisted. "It is too long, and you are using way too many words."

Happy to get the feedback, I told him, "I will work on that."

Irfan took the first shower while I worked on the Lifestory.

The Western-style commode and shower were a trial for him, as he had grown up in a rural area. When he finished, I went to take my shower. The entire bathroom was soaked. Even the toilet paper was soggy. Both towels were on the floor.

Oops, thought to myself. *Tomorrow I will go first, and I will explain to my friend how the facilities work.*

Then I called down to the front desk to find out what time their shift changed.

The operator said that it would be at eleven.

A little before eleven, I asked Irfan to go downstairs with me to see how I did telling the adjusted Lifestory to the next set of desk clerks. I told him I had cut out some of the wording and shortened it. He agreed to go and listen.

There were four people at the front desk, three men and one woman. I told them the shorter version of the Lifestory, and there was a marked difference in their responses. Their prayer was significantly more personal, and the lady was crying as she asked the Lord to come into her life. I was delighted with their responses.

On our way to the room, I thanked Irfan for the suggestions, then asked again for his opinion. "It was still boring, but it was better," he said.

I told him it was time he tried telling the Lifestory.

"Okay," he said.

I had learned at the desk that the kitchen was closed, but if we wanted a sandwich we should order it before midnight. When I got to the room, I called and placed my order, and within a few minutes there was a knock on the door.

Our room was small, but there was a table and chairs in the hallway at the top of the stairs. We decided to eat there. Once we were seated, the waiter placed the sandwich and napkins on the table before us and turned to go. "Wait," I said. "Mr. Irfan has a short story he would like to tell you. Would you like to hear it?"

"For sure," he replied.

I asked Irfan to tell him the Lifestory. It took Irfan only three minutes. I intently observed the waiter's response. He had fallen to his knees!

That's good, I thought, and I kept listening. I did not expect to hear what came next. In tears, the waiter cried out urgently, "Oh please, sir, will you stay at this hotel until I can gather my family and everyone I know to come hear this story?"

I was amazed. I interjected, "Don't forget to have him pray with you, Irfan." We then prayed with him for Jesus to come and forgive him of sin and come into his life.

As I watched this person from the local culture tell the Lifestory, God taught me two important lessons: First, keep the Lifestory short. Second, involve local people in telling the Lifestory in the local language.

I prayed for Irfan's growth and further use of the Lifestory.

What about
Follow-Up?

Almost everyone to whom we offered the Lifestory agreed to hear it. Most said yes to trusting Jesus. How would we ever follow up with them? Could we trust Jesus to shepherd them while we were away?

JESUS DID THE FOLLOW UP

What I liked best about David's response to the Lifestory was his sincere gratitude for our sharing it with him. A side benefit was the delicious sandwich, followed by a fudge brownie with vanilla ice cream. We left with a wonderful feeling of having walked with Jesus in sharing the Lifestory.

Nearly two years later, we visited Delhi again. We went to the same restaurant, hoping to see David and to enjoy another sandwich and fudge brownie. We came in through the heavy doors and were seated in an upper level. We couldn't believe what happened next.

A medium-built man crossed the room and greeted some patrons off to the left of us. By his white shirt and black dress coat, I assumed he was part of the management. I noticed that he glanced at us, then a moment later walked straight toward us.

I was a bit alarmed. We had nothing to comment on, and our food had not yet come. He stopped immediately in front of our table and asked, "Do you remember me?" At first I did not recognize him, then in a moment of shock, I realized it was David! He had grown in the last two years and was taller.

"Hello, David. How are you?" I asked.

Inside I was thanking the Lord I had remembered his name.

He spoke with us for more than fifteen minutes. In front of all the customers, he praised the name of the Lord Jesus Christ.

"I thank God for you every day in prayer. I have been walking with Jesus every day since you shared Jesus with me. He protects me from evil. No one and nothing has harmed me since you left. God has kept me from sin even though this is a little wild with music and other temptations, but God has protected me—and made me manager of this restaurant! Today I am buying your lunch! What would you like to have?"

I said, "Oh, good, we were thinking of having the fudge brownie with vanilla ice cream."

We both laughed.

"Wow! God is good! We are so happy to see you faring so well," I added.

With joined hands, we thanked God for all He has done in our lives and for David's great blessings in Jesus.

It was a real concern when we left David the first time, not knowing if we would ever see him again. But the scripture had come to mind about the Lord leaving the ninety-nine to go seek the one lost sheep, according to Luke 15:4: "What man of you, having a hundred sheep, if he loses one of them, does not leave the ninety, and, nine in the wilderness, and go after the one which is lost until he finds it?" This verse had reassured us because it wouldn't make sense to leave ninety and nine unless they were in the fold and safe.

Seeing David still walking with the Lord confirmed for us that Jesus takes care of all His sheep. We can find lost ones and trust Him to care for them, even if we cannot stay with them ourselves. We may not be able to stay with them, but God never leaves them, according to Hebrews 13:5: "For He Himself has said, 'I will never leave you nor forsake you.'"

My Start with Jesus

In 1957 Eldred Matthews was a string bean of a teenager. He was over six feet tall, while I was a short fifteen year old boy. They used to call us Mutt and Jeff.

We were good friends, maybe even best friends.

I was put to the test one day after he asked me to attend a church with him. Earlier that day, I had told him yes. Now he was at my door to collect me.

I asked my mother if I could go with him, secretly hoping she would say no. She did not.

It was just two houses from our house to the end of the block in our company town, and the edge of the ball field was across the street from that last house. It took only a few minutes to cross the field and then the main highway, which was also our main street.

Two hinged doors on the front of the church opened to the street. The right one was open, and we could hear singing inside.

We stepped into the building. Since nearly all the other seats were taken, we proceeded to the front row and sat on the far right.

The preacher gave a message about Jonah I didn't understand, but the invitation struck me right in the heart. It was about a person named Jonah who was given good instructions by God, but he ignored them and went in another direction. I thought of times I could have listened to what my Sunday school teacher told me about obeying my parents. I thought it might be negotiable. Now I was sure it was not negotiable and I did not do this? I knew something was happening to me.

In a flash, I realized I didn't have a chance to survive facing God. I felt I was condemned. The consequences of trespassing God's law were too much. What else could I do when the preacher said, "Everyone who wants to turn away from not listening to God and is ready to have God make it right and have Jesus save us from our mistakes, raise your hand."

I raised my hand.

Then he said, "Everybody who raised their hand, stand up."

I stood up.

Eldred was still seated. I grabbed his long fingers and pulled.

"Come on, Eldred. We are together on this."

Eldred got up, and I forgot about the people staring at us.

The preacher recognized us and asked if we really meant it.

I prayed silently that the preacher would not ask me about all my many sins. I feared I might wind up in reform school or the loony bin over in Orofino.

"If you really mean it, come up here and kneel." He said.

I stepped forward, and Eldred followed. We knelt before the preacher.

He asked us if we repented, and we both said yes.

I felt relieved, but I was still on guard.

Then he said, "Say this out loud: I believe Jesus Christ died for me, and I receive Him as my savior."

We obeyed.

Wow! Something fluttered in my stomach. I felt Jesus come into my being.

For the next three days, I experienced euphoria, like a warm feeling in cold weather. I felt happy and special, and I knew God loved me and had forgiven my sins.

It was nearly twenty years later that I faced the reality of having done nothing with the Lord Jesus since that moment in church.

On the inside, I knew Jesus had come to me, but on the outside, I was just like any unsaved person.

And so it was that twenty years after coming to the Lord, God sent several servants to reason together with me about turning my life over to the Lord Jesus Christ. I was compelled to follow Jesus, and this activity brought amazing changes in my life. The effect the Bible had on me, my wife, my family, and our daily lives was so wonderful. We asked Jesus to lead us. He led us into Bible college and ever onward to this day.

My first experience with Jesus when I came to Him gave me confidence that He truly is eager to come into *every* heart that will invite Him in. The second experience of being encouraged to follow Him and learning to share Him with others taught me that He is eager to lead us whenever we are ready to follow. As the old hymn says, "When we do His good will He abides with us still, and with all who will trust and obey."

THOSE YOU NEVER SEE AGAIN?

Many had said yes to trusting in Jesus, then in prayer they committed to follow Him. These people had argued vigorously with everything we had previously tried to tell them, so we could see that God was doing something. They weren't simply saying yes to please a foreigner. We felt certain that something of real eternal significance was happening.

Yet God had called us elsewhere, and we would soon be leaving this bustling city of New Delhi. There was no way we could follow up with the many who had said yes to Jesus here and in Goa.

If we had allowed our lack of ability to follow up become an excuse for not telling the Lifestory, we would have missed the great harvest God was preparing for us, and a great experience with Jesus. Who can tell what God will do through those who say yes to Jesus, even those we have no further contact with?

God was asking us to hear and follow Jesus in telling the Lifestory where laborers were lacking. We had to trust God with those who invited Jesus into their lives and committed to follow Him. We gave everyone we could the Lifestory, then trusted the Holy Spirit to guard and equip them. As we obeyed, we caught glimpses of His care for new believers, as in the story of David and the den. This confirmed our faith that we could trust God to keep all those He draws to follow Jesus. A great thing that our local tellers implemented is an amazing bible study plan that has built up the faith of their new believers. They call it His voice discipleship.

It is easy to learn to tell the Lifestory, but that is only the beginning of the spiritual battle. When God gave us the Lifestory, I committed to telling it four times a day for a month and told my wife. The devil heard this, but God also heard it. Willingness to follow Jesus was the issue. Without such a commitment, it would have been far too easy to settle for just a little more fruit rather than press through to a movement.

MOVEMENT FOLLOW UPS

We were thrilled with the responses we were seeing as we told the Lifestory, yet God had something much bigger in store than just us personally walking many through their most important decision.

Jerri and I had followed Jesus into one of the most militarized zones on earth: the disputed area between Pakistan and Northern India. This was a place where followers of Jesus were almost totally unknown. Our first years there had been nearly fruitless. Now we were headed back there with renewed vision and hope.

God clearly wants everyone to have a personal invitation to follow Jesus before they die, as recorded in Mark 16:15: "And He said to them, 'Go into all the world and preach the gospel to every creature.'" It is most effective when this invitation comes from a native of their own language and culture . Namely, someone they know and trust who can follow up with them. Someone like the woman at the well in Sychar. God began a work in such a way that corner stones were being chosen for a vast network of laborers for the harvest among the people of Kashmir?

God promised Abraham that He would bless all the family lines of earth, according to Genesis 12:3: "I will bless those who bless you, And I will curse him who curses you; And in you all the families of the earth shall be blessed." Then in Galatians 3:8: "And the Scripture, foreseeing that God would justify the Gentiles by faith, preached the gospel to Abraham beforehand, saying, 'In you all the nations shall be blessed.'"

Those who trust and follow Jesus from our personal outreach will be just a small amount compared to what is needed to win all the Lord desires. We will focus on helping people teach others to cross over to be laborers with the Gospel after they are born again.

God will do far more than give us an effective way of inviting others to follow Jesus. He will call these people to gather and present His will from the scriptures to every person who will follow Him. Our part is like being a catalyst, not a guru or a boss. We will have to respect the work God does in each person and fan the flames of their personal journey. We must move past indecision and learn to trust in Jesus the way Paul presents in Philippians 4:13: "I can do all things through Christ who strengthens me." These people will receive God's promised blessing in a way that affects the entire region. The spread of Good News will be without hesitation. Fear will be a thing of the past, and worship will be the reward. Every person will be schooled in a way to bring his or her neighbor to repent and come inside the arms of the everlasting God.

God will set the Gospel free to run among the people groups we seek to bless. God will keep and multiply those who labor and trust in Him. We will invite them to be together in their homage, and we will build them up in faith. For this, we join our counsel to their activity and our prayers for their long life.

Our lives have changed, which is clearly illustrated by 2 Corinthians 5:20: "Now then, we are ambassadors for Christ, as though God were pleading through us; we implore you on Christ's behalf, be reconciled to God."

As we returned to our home in Kashmir, we were constantly asking Jesus, "What do you want us to do next?"

In the beginning, we mostly felt He was saying, "Trust me. Take one step at a time." Now it was more definite. We were to set goals per day and per month on how many times we shared the Lifestory. We sought to duplicate tellers to increase the amount per day, then we sought to multiply by teaching tellers to teach tellers to tell and teach. Multiplication began in three months. At first it was very simple, then it became complex, as each area of the country developed in the Lord a variable sensitivity to hearing the Word.

Those we saw trained and led to trust Jesus by encouraging them constantly to be in the Word with a simple study and reply plan, eagerly learned the Lifestory and began telling it to others. It was common for them to quickly begin to tell others about the wonderful things Jesus was doing for them.

There were few Bibles available among them, and those few were shared among many new groups. Sometimes there was only one Bible. Some kissed the Bible after every gathering.

We tried buying Bibles for them, but we couldn't find enough to match the response, and it was risky to have them in public.

It was important to pray for their safety. Those who were trusting in Jesus were not hesitant about offering and telling the Lifestory to others, but most were unwilling to be seen with a Bible. Obtaining Bibles for them did not work as well as using the cell phone app.

But we experienced the Holy Spirit working deeply in those who were learning, rehearsing, and meditating on their study of the Word while they continued telling others the Lifestory. In this way, they were soaking daily in the life, death, burial, and resurrection of Jesus and His offer of eternal life. The Lifestory itself was proving to be an invaluable discipleship tool that transformed not only the hearers but also those telling it.

God led the new movement leaders to adapt local teaching patterns to give new believers competence and confidence. In just a few hours, they could train them in telling the Lifestory. This training also did something far more significant than equipping individual Lifestory tellers. The model they developed for training is done to knit each new Lifestory teller into a team with which they share continuing encouragement and accountability.

These new believers still needed a way to engage scripture without endangering themselves or their families. Using a free Bible app they could download on their smartphones, God gave them a pattern they call: His Voice Discipleship.

As Jesus guided the new movement leaders, we saw the Holy Spirit empowering them as witnesses, just as in the book of Acts.

It seemed we were rediscovering an ancient, contagious dynamic. As those new to trusting Jesus were equipped and encouraged to share what they received, their faith in Jesus was sweeping rapidly through entire households and communities. This multiplication increased their joy and accelerated their maturing. We saw the power of a faith centered on following Jesus as fishers of men and fruitful witnesses. We were learning to go with Him to seek and save the lost.

Such guidance from local leaders frees new believers from reliance on outsiders and points them toward hearing firsthand and musing over the Word of God every day. Every verse has a way to point believers to hear Jesus's voice when we ask the verse one question, which is: What question does this verse answer?

As they follow Jesus themselves, they discover that He is always with them. Many multiply thirty, sixty, or one hundredfold. Some multiply more by focusing on duplication through teaching and training.

Jesus is quoted in John 14:12: "Most assuredly, I say to you. He who believes in Me, the works that I do he will do also, and greater works than these he will do, because I go to My Father."

We think it is important that those new to trusting Jesus honor God the Father by gathering in like-minded groups. The training developed in the Kashmiri Lifestory movements facilitates readiness to act in God's stead to win the lost; grow through studying the Word; and honor God the Father, God the Son, and God the Holy Spirit with our hearts and our hands.

The Lifestory is an oral tradition of Jesus Christ for blessing all the families of the world. It spreads rapidly because the Lifestory equips local believers to lift up Jesus and invite others to hear and follow Him, and it gives them a simple way to invite their family and friends to also hear and follow Jesus and gather into a group. The groups grow in knowledge and wisdom from Christ through His Word. His personal care for everyone is evident, and it encourages each part of the body to grow in wholeness to serve everyone in the gathering. It is referenced in Ephesians 1:22,23: "And He put all things under His feet and gave Him to be head over all things to the church, which is His body, the fullness of Him who fills all in all.

LOCALS SHARING THE LIFESTORY

At first only Jerri and Jon were sharing the Lifestory, and others brought their family and friends for us to tell them the Lifestory.

Our vision needed to expand to see the vastness of the harvest and our need to involve others in sharing the Lifestory. We wondered, *How can the Lifestory bring forth more laborers for the harvest?* This question guided us as we served the Lord.

Transferring the vision is the juncture that calls for all our faith. It is the proof of divine intervention.

We have the common denominator that crosses all borders, ideologies, and religions. It Is our Lord Jesus. He does the calling, and His target is everyone. We adjust to His way and He moves the mountains and opens the doors. We are in Him according to I John 4:13: "By this we know that we abide in Him, and He in us, because He has given us of His Spirit." Together in His Word we cross into a new world of evangelism through our gain of function. The lifestorytellers is a Spiritual pandemic.

Proverbs mentions the value of a multitude of advisers. We were fortunate to have wise counselors who laughed and cried with us along the way. The Lifestory movements in North India would not have developed without their wise counsel.

Our next breakthrough to cross over came when I approached someone to be our language coach. By then it was normal for me to immediately offer the Lifestory to each new person I met, so I told him the Lifestory.

We call him Coach. Once he heard the lifestory he said: "I can hardly believe my eyes to see you and you are the answer to our prayers. For years we have asked God to send someone with a message to help us bring our friends and relatives to Jesus."

Wow! I thought. *What an important meeting!* We were impressed by the way Jesus was leading. Our new friend's ability to grasp the value of the Lifestory. It was just what we needed. He could immediately repeat the Lifestory without even a practice session. We exchanged phone numbers, and I agreed to try him as a language coach.

In those days, I rarely received any phone calls. He called me that same day. Jubilantly, he exclaimed, "I have four friends in the Kashmir Valley. I just called one of them, and he came to Jesus! I have told him about Jesus for many years, but today he heard the Lifestory and came down off the fence."

I could hear the excitement and joy in his voice.

"I just had to tell you," he continued, "and I want you to know I am calling my other three friends next to tell them the story too."

We finished the call, and I went into our house to tell Jerri the thrilling news about our future language coach and the call he had just made to one of his friends.

We wondered if this would be the connection that would take the Lifestory to the Kashmiris. Would God enable us to personally learn the language and culture and bring many to Jesus? Or would this be the beginning of something far more contagious and reproducible?

Later we received more great news from our language coach. His four friends in the upper valley had all said yes and were beginning to follow Jesus. He had encouraged them to tell the Lifestory to others, and they were doing so. They called a few days later. Now their number had grown to eleven.

They asked, "When will you send Jon to tell us more about Jesus?"

Within two weeks, this group of new believers had grown to more than sixty.

WISE COUNSEL

We called some trusted counselors and told them about the explosive growth we were starting to see and about the new believers' desire to have me come and lead a conference with as many as they could gather. They had offered to come from the valley to meet us halfway in a mountain village along the main road.

Our counselors asked a few questions about the people. I tried to answer fully. I told them they wanted Bibles in Urdu. I repeated my question: "Should I go and teach them at the conference?"

They answered, "No, do not become the guru."

I realized two things as a result: One, our counselors didn't think much of my teaching or, Two, God knows what He is doing, and He has something much bigger in mind than my exaltation as a teacher. I chose to focus on the latter reality. Jesus is the one who must be their teacher and leader.

I put away my thoughts of crafting a conference speech that would have been called something like "An Introduction to Everything." Instead, I focused on believing that the way upward was for me to decrease. It might be much more difficult than I expected, but I must follow the Lord. Other people had to become more important than myself, and I would have to become their servant. As we contemplated this, it became evident that this attitude was from the Lord and according to the scriptures.

We would have to approach our ministry in a different manner. Our altar of worship would have to be made without hands. Together, with the people here, we would lift up Jesus as our guide into all things that pertain to life and godliness. Our goal should be to encourage their progress and their application of scripture.

These people were going to have to learn the scriptures without someone from the outside spoon-feeding them. Their primary strength was their hunger for the truth. It was our assignment to introduce them to Jesus, then to stir their desire to learn more about Jesus from the scriptures and apply what they learned by sharing Him with others.

BECOME CATALYSTS

Jerri and I came to see that Jesus had called us to be catalysts serving the spread of Lifestory movements. To succeed, we needed to continually evaluate our activities and adapt ourselves to this calling. We found that this takes a lot more listening to others than we had imagined.

It is difficult to effectively cross cultural barriers. We learned that offering Jesus to those in a culture different from our own is best done by those native to that culture.

As Lifestory movement catalysts, our role became finding English speakers in an area. We would tell them the Lifestory, then enlist them to tell the Lifestory to others in their language. This proved effective, as God stirred their hearts with this simple adaptation of His Word. From our experience, it appears that Lifestory movements can easily be started anywhere. We were blessed to find Coach. He is a linguist having eight languages and a background in English literature. God set him in our midst and called him to us.

As the first Lifestory movements spread, we realized we would have to refine our call from God, examine ourselves, and eliminate nonessentials. What would we keep, and what could we put aside?

Here was our thought process: Our highest priority was to model and multiply the lordship of Jesus under the authority of scripture and the guidance of the Holy Spirit. This is crucial. It is our criteria for determining what is truly valuable and what is not. If we impart this, what more do they need from us?

The way God draws and directs us in accord with His Word decides our future; therefore the two things we value most highly are the Word of God and living in the power of Christ and the Holy Spirit's guidance.

We thus learned to ask ourselves, *To what extent are faith, hope, and love ruling our lives?* We know *what* these are, but *how are we doing* in each of these? Often I felt like Peter. Even though he stepped out on the water in faith, he began to sink. Jesus told Peter in Matthew 14:31: "And immediately Jesus stretched out His hand and caught him, and said to him, 'O you of little faith, why did you doubt?'"

Sometimes I would lie out on the grass at night praying, admitting to the Lord how little faith I had. In response, God gave me faith that if I followed Jesus among the lost like Peter did I would receive more faith. This was my process for developing more faith. I learned more of what faith was in Hebrews 11:1–2: "Now faith is the substance of things hoped for, the evidence of things not seen. For by it the elders obtained a good testimony." We prayed for a good testimony, and God helped us over and over with our faith.

I heard somewhere that faith is the sap drawn from the tree of hope. It cannot be seen or handled, but is an expectation based on God's promise that we trust to come true. Even though faith, hope, and love are quite different, they are all of the same essence, only different in status. As my faith grew, my hopes for many to follow Jesus and receive God's blessing were closer to reality. As this happened, Jesus became even more real to me, and my hope was built up. Of faith, hope, and love, love is the greatest. According to 1 Corinthians 13:13: "And now abide faith, hope, love, these three; but the greatest of these is love." I feel introducing others to Jesus refines my love.

Peter was unsure of his faith after denying Jesus three times. This is where I, too, find myself lacking, even though I know He is with me.

Peter was guided by Jesus to examine himself and to love others without worrying about his past. God confronted me by bringing to my mind again a statement I once applied from musing either from thought or memory of another's idea: "We only love God as much as we love the person we hate the most."

We love best when God loves through us because God is love. After His resurrection, Jesus helped Peter realize he needed a stronger, deeper love to succeed in the next step of his calling.

During our search for purpose, love becomes the final litmus test in recognizing our calling. Love requires us to elevate others and to consider it a gift to serve them for Jesus.

As we continued to evaluate our role in the Lifestory movement, at times the path forward seemed impossible. When we were originally called to build a road in an impossible-looking place, we thought our own ability was most important. When we were called to introduce people to Jesus in a place where little response seemed possible, we considered our religious background most important. But we came to realize we were weak in ourselves. It's a good thing God is always greater than our weakness!

As it turned out, neither our ability nor our religious background mattered. We could never bring salvation to the vast number who needed Jesus. We could only bring faith to another because we believed it was possible through God. We could only show what is invisible to someone because hope is alive in us. Loving another as God loves us was far beyond our ability, but God is not finished with us. Little by little, He is making us clean. God's work in us draws others to Himself.

Our goal, like that of our many like, minded friends, is to approach everyone with love and respect as we help them encounter Jesus and make a decision to follow Him. When we succeed, we are not just attaining a goal; we are becoming co-laborers and deliverers of eternal life through Jesus. Lifestory movements fulfill this goal. It is an oral tradition of Jesus Christ for blessing all the families of the world.

Something was happening. A dream was becoming reality and it was a dream of an ever growing number of Lifestory teams and Lifestory movements that faithfully obey the Lord in going to all and being fruitful and multiplying.

From what we saw in telling the Lifestory and in the reactions of those deciding to trust Jesus, we realized that Lifestory movements would have a major effect on both our lives and the people we were called to serve.

And whom are we called to serve? Anyone we talk to is a potential believer and labourer for the harvest. We are the servant of everyone who says yes to Jesus and promises to follow Him.

LIFESTORY TELLER TEACHERS

As the *Lifestory* movement grew, we could no longer provide all the training. Believers *within* the movement needed to become the teachers for the many new Lifestory tellers.

A New Leader of a New Movement

Our language coach came to our house. By this time, we were simply calling him Coach.

It was a thrill to hear how the Lifestory was spreading within his circle of friends in the Kashmir Valley. They were planning to hold a conference, convinced that it was needed to bring more unity among the different families who had trusted Jesus. They wanted to discuss Jesus and to hear more about Him from the Word.

The conference was going to happen soon. As I was not going to be the "guru," they still needed an emcee. As we prayed for someone to lead, I sensed God reminding me of a statement that helped us many times while beginning the Lifestory movement: "Stop praying for something you already have."

We lifted our heads, and I looked at Coach. He looked back. We had both heard God say that Coach would lead the event. Coach "wobbled" his head in the Indian way to say yes. We were ready to trust God together for the needs of these who were new to trusting Jesus.

Having agreed that Coach would emcee, he still wanted my advice about what should he say? We prayed about it and decided he would start with this question: "What are some good things that have happened since you asked Jesus to come into your life?"

He would then moderate the discussion. The attendees would also be encouraged to read portions of the scripture and pray for God's love and peace to stay with them as they continued to share Jesus.

Coach's report after the conference was a delight to hear. People had reported many miracles that Jesus had done among them.

I wanted to encourage Coach in his work with appropriate praise.

Part of my duty as a catalyst is to applaud their success at following the Lord.

It is important that those who proclaim the Lifestory be dreaming and hoping that a movement will develop.

I reminded Coach of the way Jesus was building the movement up for things yet to come. "Just look at what God has done with you and the Lifestory. Until this conference, we had only a few people telling the Lifestory. Now we also have a conference speaker, a conference organizer, and other workers praising the Lord together. Thanks to Jesus and you, we have taken another step forward with Jesus and the Lifestory."

Coach was grinning. I was too, as I knew he would pass on my words of encouragement to the folks in the valley. We were beginning to experience a growing movement for the Lord!

We had discovered a key to open a door that had been locked. We now would introduce Jesus from within the culture. We now think movements should be started by local people who are born again and convinced by the voice of Jesus, through the Word of God and His Holy Spirit, to witness openly in every place. For the movement to multiply, it was essential that God be the one who would bring Jesus to them. Our role would become one of simply coaching the new leaders.

New Life in a Motorcade

Tuesday was a new day. After our morning lesson, Coach left to walk home. As he neared the highway bypass, a motorcade approached. A number of soldiers on motorcycles came first, then the main vehicle. Several more soldiers rode behind.

Coach looked up from his position on the sidewalk. The windows of the car were tinted, and he could not see who was inside. To his surprise, the motorcade stopped beside him. He was about to break and run—a reaction learned amid his violent past in the valley. But one of the soldiers shouted toward him, "The official wishes to talk with you."

His heart quickened.

"Would you please be so kind as to lower the window so I can see who it is?"

As the window opened, Coach saw the smiling face of an old school chum. Let's call him M. Awan, though that is not his real name.

M. Awan motioned Coach forward. He approached and grasped the hand of his old friend. "I am requesting that you have a cup of tea with me," M. Awan said.

Coach replied, "Yes, I would be pleased. I would also like to tell you a short story."

"Of course, you can tell me lots of stories if you like."

They parked the motorcade and entered a nearby restaurant. Even the guards came with their rifles. They all listened to Coach tell the Lifestory. When Coach asked M. Awan about trusting Jesus to save him, he said yes, as did the soldiers with him.

From their hearts came the prayer that sealed the agreement in heaven and earth. They would trust Jesus, He would save them, and they would follow Him.

Being a man of action, M. Awan then requested time to make a phone call. The officer who picked up the phone heard a peculiar request. "Can you listen?" he asked.

The officer answered, "You have my attention."

M. Awan told him the Lifestory. The officer prayed and became a new believer. The officer's next words were, "Will you excuse me? I would like to call my wife and tell her this story immediately."

Coach's obedience to Jesus resulted in eternal life for many that day.

M. Awan had this to say: "As a public servant in this area, I have lived in fear for my life every day until now. I am so grateful to find this peace with Jesus."

Through M. Awan, we came to see the selfless courage that civic leaders show in serving the people of this country.

We always watch for our next step with Jesus and the Lifestory movements. Our goal is to know that we are following Jesus every moment of every day. We study the Word every day, and we listen for His voice. As a result, milestones seem to be passing like fence posts on a rural highway.

THE EDITOR

We determined we needed copies of the Lifestory in Urdu. Coach had translated it, and we needed it printed. Coach took me to the home of the editor of one of the largest newspapers in the city. He dropped me off, promising to return in a short while.

I rang the bell at the front gate and waited. The gate slid open with the hum of an electric motor. Summoning me to the front porch with the wave of his hand, the editor seemed in a hurry to greet me. I removed my shoes, according to the local custom, and entered the house, closing the bug screen on the way.

Inside were several overstuffed easy chairs facing a TV. The editor sat in one of the chairs, engrossed in old reruns of a US comedy show. I sat for a moment and went over our priority list: follow Jesus, introduce others to Jesus, and do the work of a Lifestory movement catalyst.

I could not sit any longer. I was sure the editor needed salvation, so that would come first. I decided to ask him about printing the Lifestory for us.

"Excuse me, sir! Would you mind turning off the TV? I have something to tell you, and it's more important than anything else."

The show was finished, so the editor got up and turned off the set. I told him the Lifestory. He looked up to Jesus and trusted Him to save him from his sins. He was touched, and he cried.

Then we discussed the publication and printing. He said, "I can edit the Lifestory and prepare it for printing by tomorrow, but we are an Islamic news organization, and I can only add it to the paper as a paid advertisement."

I gave him the copy of the Lifestory that Coach had prepared. He explained he wouldn't charge us for editing, but publishing the Lifestory would require paying a weekly amount to the paper. He felt it would be better not to do that. I listened to his reason and agreed to hold off on that idea.

We shook hands, and I slipped on my shoes and left through the electric-powered gate. No taxi was there, so I waited. Thinking back on the interaction, I realized I really liked the editor. He showed a sense of purpose and organization that fit together well. In the future, we would receive lots of help from the paper and staff. Soon the taxi with Coach appeared. I hopped in, and we continued on to my home.

Jon Smith

First Lifestory Teacher Training

Some days later, Coach told me seven men from the northern Kashmir Valley were coming to be trained in properly telling the Lifestory.

They had felt God's Spirit enter them when they trusted in Jesus. They wanted to learn more and to ensure that they were telling the Lifestory properly. Their need for training would guide us to the next step in following Jesus with the Lifestory.

These men were from three different languages, so the training would be complicated by the need for translation. I felt nervous but confident that Jesus would guide us. Fortunately, Coach was a language instructor fluent in all these languages and several more.

These men were all Muslims with zealous hearts. All were in their early to midtwenties. They would be coming into our home, so preparations were necessary. Our challenge would be to teach them, feed them, and be good hosts without offending them.

Coach explained that only paper plates and cups could be used because of their sensitivity about eating from plates or utensils that may have had contact with pork. It was also advised, as much as possible, that we serve food that had been prepared and packaged, like chips and dips and such. Fresh veggies were also good.

We found a silver pitcher and bowl to hold water for the guests to wash with before eating and provided a clean linen towel to dry with. Also, we would all need to dress appropriately.

Several weeks later, the seven men arrived. Coach was waiting there with me, and he invited them to come in and sit for tea.

These men were as diverse looking as could be. One stood out, with curly black hair and a full, dark beard. I learned he had walked 25 miles through deep snow to come to the training; then the group had traveled over 185 miles along a narrow highway in steep, rugged country and harsh weather.

This was an important training, and I was not to be the teacher. We were their servants, and Coach was their teacher.

Their response to the training was simple. Shah, the curly-haired man with the beard, stood and said, "We must complete this mission."

We loved them and fed them the best we could. Before they departed, we prayed. I personally was honored to pray for each of them. We gave them a little cash for the trip back and bid them farewell.

Back in Jammu,[1] reports came in about the progress of those who took the training at our house. Shah went back to his home with a fire burning in his heart. He gathered fifteen men to accompany him through the deep snow to his cabin in the mountains. Within a week, they had taken in the Lifestory as part of their new life in Jesus. They then made plans to carry the Lifestory movement into the highest regions of Kashmir.

God had shown us that training Lifestory tellers and Teachers of Lifestory tellers would be a major part of the Lifestory movements. Today I am awestruck by who these men have become and what the Lord has done through them. All these seven extended the Lifestory movement beyond what we could have asked or imagined. More than one laid down their life in the course of doing so.

---

[1] Jammu is the largest city in the Jammu Division and the winter capital of the state of Jammu and Kashmir in India. It is on the banks of the Tawi River.

DEVELOPING TEAMS

Soon new believers were gathering in teams to support, challenge, and encourage one another in spreading Lifestory movements in their own communities and other communities.

Lifting Jesus Higher

Shah and Arjand assembled a team from the Aknoor area for a high elevation expedition. They wanted to take the Lifestory to a village in the Kargil area. All were committed to do whatever it would take to succeed in their "fisher of men" project. Several places they planned to visit were predominantly Buddhist, others were Muslim, but it was unlikely that any had ever heard the good news about salvation.

All the Lifestory tellers were leaving the comforts of home and their livelihoods in order to help others come into the safety of having the perfect savior, who is the Christ. Shah would be leaving his ranch untended, which could mean little or no harvest in the fall. But Shah and all those with him had their eyes on a bigger harvest in a higher place.

Some of the men had relatives and friends in the area. This would be a great help in finding shelter and supplies for the team.

They began their journey and their mission in the spring, after the main road was cut open through drifts of snow more than a hundred feet deep.

Their plan was simple. They would arrive in Ladakh, start with known relatives, and tell the Lifestory to everyone who would listen.

When they arrived, Majeed found his uncle and brought him into the fellowship. His uncle became an anchor for them and the teams to come. He owned a shop on the main street and dedicated it to the Lifestory tellers. It has become a meeting place and a house of prayer for Lifestory tellers on a mission. It now bears the sign "Lifestory Station."

An amazing young Buddhist priest became a fellow fisher of men. His father and mother were well-known servants in the main temple. They took the first team into their home and made them welcome in their community. It was a perfect open door for the good news.

The team stayed into the beginning of winter. Running low on supplies, they started back to their homes in the valley. Upon arrival at his ranch, Shah was at a loss for what to do. It was one month after the harvest season, but he would have to harvest something to meet expenses for the winter.

Shah called in his friends and all the Lifestory tellers who could come. The harvest began, and all worked hard. Optimistically, he ordered his usual two trucks to haul the crop to Delhi—nearly six hundred miles away. The harvesters readily filled the two trucks with more than enough crop to fill another truck. This was a truckload more than Shah had ever harvested!

While the trucks went to Delhi, some expressed concern about the crop being over-ripe. Another said that because the harvest was so late the price might be too low to even pay for the trucking. A request for prayer was circulated, and Lifestory tellers in many places prayed for the harvest to be blessed by God.

Then word came to Shah. Because the shipment was far later than all the other shippers, there would indeed be a change in price, but there was no mention of an overripe crop.

Shah waited for their decision. Finally, he learned that the earlier supply had run out, and there was great need for his produce. Because his crop arrived so late, he received a price three times higher than he had ever received!

He had miraculously received three times as much and for a third more crop. Everyone rejoiced with Shah. The Lord was rejoicing also. Shah is a giving person, and this was a good life lesson for all the Lifestory tellers in Kashmir.

Shepherds

Rafan, one of my good friends from our time in the Srinagar area, is a shepherd of shepherds. I worked alongside him while he was helping to bring veterinary medicine to the migratory clans in the mountain areas of Kashmir. He is part of a very large group of nomads who range throughout many countries.

I found these people to be fearless, warmhearted, cunning, unselfish, loving, and hopefully optimistic about life. They may be stirred to anger, but so rarely that I never saw it. They travel through lonely forests and over awesome high mountains, past rushing cold streams and among fierce and deadly predators. They also talk on a personal level to an amazing number of people each year.

I think my anthropologist friends would be interested in the last trait. Here is how I discovered it. Rafan and I became friends from the first day we worked together. I soon learned he had come to Jesus when a servant of the Lord had previously visited the area.

I was visiting the area of Srinagar for a few weeks, and Rafan came to see me at my rented apartment not far from his tent. I told the Lifestory to him and got a good reaction. "Would you like to be able to share this story with your family?" I asked.

"How can I learn this?"

I told him, "I will teach you. I will start tonight, and we will finish tomorrow night after your work is finished." He agreed, and I started to teach him the Lifestory.

As we had arranged, Rafan came back the next night and finished learning the Lifestory. He also told me he was trying to replace his phone.

This gave me an idea. I knew he would soon migrate into the highlands. What if I could help him with his phone, and he could help me document how his Gujjar Bakarwal people responded to the Lifestory when it was presented by one of their own?

I told Rafan that for the next few months he could do something that would help me and also be a blessing to him. If he would keep records as he told the Lifestory by writing the name and phone number of each person he told the Lifestory to and whether they said yes or no to Jesus then I would pay him two rupees (a little more than two cents) per name for these records.

Rafan looked at me stoically for about ten seconds, then said: "Okay. You give me paper."

I gave him a medium-sized lined notebook and a copy of the Urdu Lifestory. We parted ways, and I did not see him again for several months. Later I returned to Srinagar and rented the same apartment for a week.

A special guest named Suebee was with us, working on her thesis for a master's degree in anthropology. She was also in training to tell the Lifestory.

Rafan came to the door, and I invited him in. We greeted each other warmly and traded questions about how our families were doing. I asked about the health of everyone, including the dogs and other animals. He had a cloth purse hanging from his neck. An impish smile came over his face as he pulled out some worn pieces of paper.

He had kept records just as I had asked when we parted company. Each name had a date when that person heard the Lifestory from Rafan. The response of yes or, the response of no, was recorded directly after the name. Most had a yes, but a few were no. Many also had phone numbers. The total number of people he recorded telling the Lifestory to that summer was over eleven hundred! I owed him twenty-two hundred rupees (thirty-two dollars), and I was elated.

All the people on Rafan's list were men. I learned from these records that shepherd men in Rafan's clan don't often have lengthy conversations with women outside their immediate family. To overcome this, we would have to do something differently.

To my knowledge, no one had ever been paid to tell the Lifestory, and this was essential to protect against local communities wrongly thinking people were being paid to convert. I don't believe it wise or helpful to ever offer payment for telling the Lifestory. But I do believe Jesus led me to pay Rafan for record keeping as the movement spread where I could not safely go. These records proved very helpful to us.

Rafan became a renowned Lifestory teller among the clans. He is often called upon to tell the Lifestory at weddings and in meetings with this shepherd people. He has organized teams of Lifestory tellers among his friends and family, and he cares for widows and orphans. We count it a great honor to be accepted as his friend. We look forward with him for God's blessing in Jesus to come to all the people of Kashmir.

Bakarwal widows summer camp near road to Ladak

Introducing Women to Jesus

Suebee, who knew the shepherd Gojri language, made plans with my wife, Jerri, to tell the Lifestory to Gojri speaking women. Suebee had already intended to visit these shepherds as part of her studies, and to refresh her own relationship with these dear people. We thought it would be good for them to start with Rafan's mother and sisters, as they were camped on the hillside just outside of town.

The next morning, Jerri and Suebee trekked up the rocky trail to the shepherd's camp. They were invited into the tents and served *roti* which is an Indian flatbread cooked on a blackened flat iron. They also received *numkin chai* which is salty tea with goat's milk and brewed over a small homemade clay stove.

After some conversation, Suebee told the Lifestory. All the women said yes to Jesus and prayed, asking Him to save them and come into their lives. This was a small beginning to something amazing.

The next day, after sharing in the camp, Suebee and Jerri made appointments to meet with a hairdresser and a seamstress. Both meetings brought about opportunities to tell the Lifestory, both times with great results. The seamstress lived in a nice, large home with her son, not far from the trail to the shepherd camp. Her husband had recently been killed in an auto accident. It was very hard for her to live with her deep sorrow. The Lord's gentle hand was on her when she received Him as her savior, and she wanted us to know she was very grateful to have God come and comfort her.

Fortunately, she was a very good English speaker. She invited us over to tell the Lifestory to her cousins and her son. We obeyed the Lord and told them the Lifestory. Her cousins came willingly to the Lord. I tried to befriend the son, but he was deeply troubled over losing his dad. He had questions about God and life that would not be solved in a different language nor in a short time.

Our friend Suebee went on to become a professor. While we were in Srinagar, she received a call from a university assuring her of a position there. We rejoiced together. Later she married and now has a wonderful family. The shepherds will never forget Suebee.

First Widows' Team

We began to realize that noticing and meeting peoples' needs was an essential part of organizing and motivating expansion of the Gospel. Addressing the needs of widows and orphans is a high priority. We aspire to lift widows to a position of honor, recognizing their contribution to life in the family and the clan as they face the difficult challenge of raising children in a harsh environment. They are courageous, and it is common for them to be among the first to learn and use the Lifestory.

There are many widows among the shepherds because their life is dangerous. At night they guard their goats, sheep, and horses against bears and leopards. Even the dogs that help watch over the flock live in great danger. They have little defense because it is not legal to harm the predators.

I visited a camp one day when four of their dogs had been eaten by a leopard. The shepherds face the same danger, as seen by the scars on their bodies and faces.

Currently five widows with children are under Rafan's care. He has worked very hard to help them, such as making their homes sturdier. As I write this, however, these widows are facing a setback, as others with influence want the widows' land for their own use. Would you pray for these widows? Their leader has four children. All the children of these widows experience God's blessing in Jesus and survive serious difficulties with the Lord's help.

These widows draw strength from God's Word. They are great Lifestory tellers, and many otheres are listening to the Lifestory as a result.

There are other teams of women and widows. We have found them to be pleasant and beautiful people, honorable in the eyes of the Lord. We thank them all for being a part of the great success the Lord is giving to the Lifestory tellers in Kashmir.

For example, an elderly lady told the Lifestory to a man who was so harsh and unforgiving no one could approach him. He repented and became a lovely man of grace.

One group of widows in a remote place desperately needed supplies. Yet if a man were to bring support to a widow, it could ruin her reputation. One of the widows solved the problem by entering the area herself. She brought the needed supplies, along with a good supply of loving comfort. By the time she left to return home, the ladies were calling her Mother.

The Bible says he who gives to the poor, including widows and orphans, lends to the Lord. This is found in: Proverbs 19:17: "He who has pity on the poor lends to the Lord, And He will pay back what he has given."

Surprise, a New Team

Six men came to us from the valley, making their way through the worst violence in many years. They each learned the Lifestory and made a commitment to continue to tell it. They wanted us to confirm them as a team.

We needed them, they needed us, and we all need Jesus. They were two each from three cities—Shopian, Pahalgam, and Srinagar. Three were Kashmiris and three shepherds, each less than six months old in Jesus, yet with a passion to share with others the gift they had received. Some had heard the Lifestory over the phone, and some had had it presented to them in person by a Lifestory teller.

They agreed to form a team and call themselves the Firebrands. One of them said, "The Lifestory is so good to share that we can start in the morning and by evening have a new group of people willing to follow Jesus." Some shared how they had been chased after curfew, evading capture so they could come and be with us for a moment.

When followers of Islam pray, they turn at one point to the right shoulder and then to the left, addressing the recording angels there, *"As-Salaam-Alaikum."* This means "Peace be with you," and it is done five times every day. According to Islamic tradition, the angel on the right shoulder records their good deeds, and the angel on the left records their bad deeds. This is a ritual they all know and are used to doing in the mosque.

When one of the men in our training took off his jacket, a written copy of the Lifestory was visible, neatly folded and placed strategically on his left shoulder to remind him he is free. There are no more chains to his sins of the past, just more of Jesus.

Our time with these men was over too soon. They left by a side door, carefully watching for those who might pursue them. This group of six became one of the first Lifestory teams.

One Leader's Challenges

The Lifestory movement had already spread to nomadic shepherds. Now one fruitful leader experienced great fruitfulness and significant opposition.

MESSENGER D'S BEGINNING

One person at that first training was Messenger D was a slender man with short brown hair and a serious smile. We are so thankful for every second he was with us. When it came to following Jesus, I felt he was a kindred spirit. It was an honor to pray for him that day and many days since as he lived out his life in Jesus. Below are ways in which God blessed Messenger D as a Lifestory movement leader.

On a cold fall day, just before the first snow, Messenger D, his cousin, and a friend traveled toward Frozen Lake. They were going to attend another cousin's wedding. Messenger D had heard his family had banished him because he was actively sharing Jesus. His attempt to attend the wedding would reveal whether this was true.

Messenger D and his companions came into the courtyard of the home where the wedding was to take place and were met at the door. They asked Messenger D to leave. His two companions stayed with him and shared his sorrow as they walked back down the road toward town.

It was getting cold. There were plenty of trees and brush, so they built a good fire just off the road. Snow was starting to fall, lightly at first but increasing as night approached. Although he was thankful he wasn't alone, Messenger D wanted his friend and cousin to attend the wedding without him. Instead, they sat with him around the fire.

Messenger D's friend pulled a pack of cigarettes from his shirt, lit one, and began to smoke. Messenger D saw him. Remembering something he had read in the Bible, Messenger D said, "According to the Bible, we are God's temple. It hurts me to see you harm your temple, because it belongs to Jesus."

His friend said, "Messenger D, if it hurts your feelings, I will do this no more." He then threw the lit cigarette into the fire. Reaching into his pocket, he removed the pack and threw it into the flames too.

For a while all was quiet, then they heard the clatter of horse's hooves and saw a cart approaching. The couple in the cart knew Messenger D. As they were going the same way, they offered him a ride. He climbed into the cart, and both his friend and his cousin bid him farewell and headed back to the wedding. God was transforming Messenger D into His messenger, giving him an unstoppable commitment to tell the Lifestory to every person who would hold still long enough to hear it. Thus the man and his wife in the cart became some of the first in this area to hear the Gospel.

They had traveled only a short distance before Messenger D began telling the Lifestory. He had done this so many times before that it was natural for him to make the Lifestory the first part of every conversation with anyone who might not have heard it yet. Because of his passion for delivering the Lord's message, forty-two families living along this road would hear the Lifestory and begin to follow Jesus.

When Messenger D reached his own home back in the valley, he had been out of town for several days. His son and daughters were happy to see him, but his wife ignored him, as she had lately begun doing. He thought that maybe this was because he was following Jesus. She did not seem to be interested in his involvement with the Lifestory movement. But when she complained of stomach pains, he took her to a doctor and found that she was having a problem with her gallbladder. No wonder she was distant; she was in pain!

There is a Muslim hospital on the North side of Srinagar. Messenger D's wife was in the community ward waiting for an infection to decrease so they could operate on her gallbladder. He was visiting her in the ward and preparing to tell her the Lifestory.

On a nearby bed lay another lady who was quite young. Her name was Jasmin. Her situation was serious, and she seemed only partially conscious. She was attended by her older brother. Messenger D asked Jasmin's brother if it would be all right for her to hear the story also, assuming that she could hear at all. He said yes.

As Messenger D told the Lifestory, he hesitated every now and then because Jasmin seemed to mumble something under her breath.

Near the end of the Lifestory, Messenger D came to the part where it was time to trust Jesus to forgive and to save, and for the listener to call to Him with a yes. Messenger D's wife confirmed she would trust Jesus to save her; then Jasmin called for the nurse and asked to sit up. She said that something had just happened to her.

"What happened to you?" the nurse asked.

"I don't know, but I am better. I think I am well! I just trusted Jesus to save me. He reached out to me, and now I am okay."

Jasmin was soon released from the hospital with no further treatment. When she arrived at her village, they asked her about her meeting with Jesus. She told them all she could about it and then referred them to Messenger D so they could hear first hand the story he was telling. This was such a dramatic event for the village that they insisted on finding Messenger D. When he came, he was confident they would all respond positively to the Lifestory. They were so excited and happy that God was with them that they tried to change the name of their village to Village of Miracles.

In Prison You Came

Several days after Jasmin left the hospital, Messenger D's wife was operated on for her gallbladder. After her recuperation, Messenger D went to the city and inquired at the jail. He wanted to check on the well being of some prisoners he knew and tell them the Lifestory.

Messenger D was only permitted to see a few prisoners. Among the prisoners was M. Dard, who was considered a terrorist and a threat to society. He hated other religions and tried to burn down their temples. He had been sentenced to many years in that dreadful prison.

Messenger D entered the prison and began to share with a few men. It was dark and cold, and the men looked haggard and forlorn. As he shared the Lifestory, they appeared to be savouring every word. As he neared the end, they were clearly hoping for more. When it came time to look up to Jesus the Lord, they were shocked to realize He had come for them inside their prison. Today was their day of salvation, and they all trusted in Him. M. Dard was saved.

MESSENGER D AND SHEPHERDS

It was late spring in the valley. The hills were green with grass, and the surrounding peaks were sharing the water from their blanket of snow with the streams and rivers below. Some shepherds were minding their flocks near the towns and villages.

It was customary for them to use the hungry sheep and goats to trim the roadsides and the edges of the irrigation ditches. Soon they would be moving on to faraway places well beyond the imagination of the local occupants. Messenger D thought to himself, *These shepherds need the Lord.*

A band of shepherds was ranging nearby, above the town, so one evening he walked to their camp. He tried to talk with them, but they claimed they were too busy to talk with him. In reality, the people were suspicious. Still, they gave him tea and roti.

Shepherds near Messenger D

He came back to them the next day and then the next. Still they claimed they were too busy for any conversation. Stubbornly, Messenger D followed them. He would not let up until they would let him tell them the Lifestory. He followed them into the mountains. In the evening, they shared their tea and bread, and Messenger D slept on the ground.

The next bright morning, when they were loading their mules and donkeys and preparing to leave, one of them signaled to Messenger D to come over to a large stone. The other men of the clan joined them there. "You cannot come with us any further," the man said. "You must tell us what you have on your mind, because we cannot sleep."

Messenger D told the Lifestory in the language of the shepherds, and they were elated to hear it! They said yes and promised to follow Jesus. Instead of fearing Messenger D, they began to follow him.

He told them more about Jesus, then bid them farewell and started for home. He soon realized they were right behind him. Walking up to the man who had first addressed him, Messenger D put his hand on the man's chest and said, "He is in here, and he will stay here. When you pray, he will help you! Jesus the Christ loves you. That is why He will not leave you."

The man replied, "If you love us, why are you leaving?"

Messenger D could see this was going to be difficult. He couldn't have these people ruining their migration plans to be with him. He kept trying to leave their camp without them following. It took several days for Messenger D to convince them that even if he left them Jesus would never leave them. Jesus would still be with them always. Finally, the leader came to him again and said, "You will go without us because you are a very determined person, and we cannot win over you."

They shook hands, hugged each other, and spoke the customary farewell. Messenger D quickly retreated down the mountain trail and out of sight.

Trouble for Messenger D.

Trouble was brewing for Messenger D. As his close friends, each of us would suffer along with him. He told the Lifestory so often it brought him notoriety. Those in the mosque accepted malicious gossip against him and labeled him a blasphemer. His home was attacked, and his life was threatened. His son, two daughters, and wife were urged to leave him.

This was frightening for all of us, and we feared for the safety of all Lifestory tellers. We loved Messenger D's passion for telling the Lifestory, yet we were concerned. Could a balance be found to keep the peace?

Reaction against Messenger D would affect all the Lifestory tellers, but conflict appeared inevitable. We asked the Lord for wisdom to overcome the impending clash between the way things have always been done there and the way, the truth, and the life.

We prayed. The team decided that leadership of the Firebrands must be passed to another for a time. Firdoo was elected to lead the groups, freeing Messenger D to address the challenges in his personal life. We would all support him the best we could.

Messenger D's wife went to work in the young moulvi's[2] sewing factory. The young moulvi convinced her that his ideology was the correct one, strongly encouraging her and her extended family to denounce Messenger D as the family leader and to keep away from him. His two daughters cried to stay with Messenger D, but their mother took them to her parent's home. His house was dark and empty.

---

[2] Moulvi (also spelled "maulvi," "mawlawi," and "mawlvi") is an honorific Islamic religious title given to Muslim religious scholars.

The moulvi was suspicious and outspoken against Messenger D's activities, accusing Messenger D of blasphemy and warning him that he was going to do something about it. One day the Moulvi gathered the panchayat.[3] He asked them to order Messenger D to appear for an inquisition to determine if Messenger D was blaspheming the masjid and their holy prophet. The punishment for this was death by hanging.

We notified the team leaders in our area and began to fast and pray. Coach and I were on the roof, just about to begin a Lifestory training seminar for thirteen men and women, when his cell phone rang. Messenger D spoke to him in worried tones. Turning to me, Coach reported, "He is asking us what to do when they ask about the Lifestory?" We agreed that he should tell the truth.

Messenger D's interrogation would last more than eight hours. He was nervous and cautious, not wishing to cause any problems for the Lifestory tellers. We felt that everything would turn out well; it did not seem possible that God would let him down. We prayed for his protection and for wisdom on how he could show the panchayat the truth without creating conflict with the established faith. Messenger D was not against the faith of Islam. He was for Jesus.

---

[3] Panchayat. Five elders who preside over domestic concerns in a village or town.

JON SMITH

Prayer and Training

They called us to start the training, and we came down off the roof. We kept our cell phones close in case word came. A judgment against Messenger D would increase the danger for all the Lifestory Tellers, and many of the leaders knew Messenger D or had been praying for him.

We held Messenger D up in prayer with one hand and taught the new Lifestory tellers with the other. Like rising floodwaters, the situation was out of our control. There wasn't much we could do about it but pray. The suspicion against Messenger D had become so strong that we could not go there and try to rescue him without compounding the problem. Messenger D was in danger, and our intervention could lead to more difficulty for all the Lifestory tellers.

We waited and continued praying. Hour after hour went by with no word from him. We could only imagine the pressure and the pain he must be enduring, being accused in front of his hometown. It was getting late, so we closed the training for the day. We headed across town in silence, waiting in vain for the phone to ring.

It was late that evening when we finally heard from Messenger D. When Coach answered the phone, I went to my knees again and prayed in my heart for God to deliver him.

It was such relief to see a smile on Coach's face!

Coach asked: "Do you mean to say you are free now?" he verified: "Yes I am free."

God had answered our prayers. Opening my palms and lifting my arms toward heaven, I shouted, "Yes, Lord! Yes!"

This was a major milestone for the Lifestory, fostering a more positive relationship between the Lifestory tellers and their neighbors. Messenger D had passed the inquisition. The Lifestory is like the great second chance offered by God to desperate people. It could now continue to be shared by the people of Kashmir.

A Day With Messenger D

The inquisition of Messenger D had gone something like this: He was summoned to his in-laws' home. There he was met by a large crowd, including his wife's parents, other family members, and the village panchayat. In addition, one moulvi and some other clerics accused Messenger D of blasphemy and of spreading Christianity more than Islam. Finally, a person was present who must remain unnamed. He held the position of highest authority and was the only one there with a gun.

Messenger D was frightened, and we were praying for him. Just before he entered the meeting his friends again advised, "Don't fear; trust in Jesus. Whatever they ask, answer honestly and clearly."

The inquisition began. Messenger D was asked hundreds of questions about his faith and beliefs. Loud accusations came from the excited in-laws and the moulvi. The moulvi asked some locals, and even Messenger D's wife, to testify. No one would testify that he was guilty of outright blasphemy toward the mosque or against the prophet, who is blessed. Rather, all the testimony involved suspicion and hearsay.

The clergy and Messenger D's family stated that he spent more time talking about the prophet Jesus than anything else. This was permitted, even in the masjid, but it was agreed that he should talk much more about their beloved Mohammad, peace be upon him.

The moulvi asked, "Why is he acting this way? Why should he be allowed to be so different?"

Messenger D was shaken. It was late in the day, and no decision had been made. The man who was carrying the rifle spoke up, asking Messenger D if he was a believer.

Messenger D said, "Why do you ask if I am a believer in Islam?"

The man replied, "Because everyone in the area is saying you have denounced your faith and are following Christianity."

Messenger D responded, "How could I denounce my faith? When I was born, it was told in my ear to love Allah and to follow the prophet and obey the prophets. I have never denounced or blasphemed Allah or any of the prophets. I believe as I always have believed, and I believe in Jesus.[4]

Messenger D. told them: "No person can say in truth that I have blasphemed against the mosque. I will offer myself to be hanged in the *masjid* if anyone can prove that I have."

With this, the one carrying rifle shook his head and declared, "If what this man has said is true, what are you doing with his wife and family in your home?"

His eyes went to the inlaws, and then to the *Moulvi*. Turning to address everyone, he then stated with authority, "I believe Messenger D is telling the truth. From now on there will be someone watching over his home. No one is to harm him or his family." The Muslim clerics were nodding their heads in approval.

The inquisition was over.

As Messenger D walked home with his wife and children, the *Moulvi* walked beside him, and his wife walked behind the Moulvi. He said, "Can you tell me what you are saying about the Prophet Jesus?"

Messenger D. explained: "I tell a story. I will tell you, if you agree?"

"I agree," said the *Moulvi*.

Messenger D told him the complete Lifestory, and the moulvi received it completely. He said yes to Jesus and prayed for forgiveness. Just like those who looked up to the serpent on the pole, he trusted Jesus to save him. He also told Messenger D that he saw something new about God.

---

[4] This is how the Holy Spirit led David to be "wise as a serpent" during his interrogation. The New Testament lifts up Jesus much more than it argues against other belief systems. Lifestory tellers follow suit.

When Messenger D arrived home, the street was littered with his clothes and dishes. An emotional group of rioters had come through during the questioning. All his windows were broken, and his garden was destroyed. This was the price Messenger D paid for being under suspicion. Heaven has the bill for this, and compensation is guaranteed. We were thankful for the government presence that kept the damage from being worse.

Training More Lifestory Tellers

Following the wisdom of local believers regarding the training process has been essential to the development of Lifestory leaders.

LIFESTORY TRAINING RESUMES

While Messenger D was with the moulvi, Coach and I were running a two day training seminar. The last item on the agenda was for the trainees to practice telling the Lifestory to someone, then regroup to share what they liked best about the responses.

We sent them out in two-person teams. Each one would approach a person and offer them the Lifestory. When they got to the question asking if that person would trust Jesus to save them, they were to wait for a yes or no answer. They would then pray with any person who said yes. They would also offer to pray for the person who said no.

One would tell the Lifestory while the other would pray. The one praying would be ready to help in case the Lifestory teller forgot a part or became distracted. The helper would only speak up if the Lifestory teller paused for ten seconds or more. It took close to an hour for most to complete the exercise and meet back together. Coach asked, "What did you like best about the response you received to the Lifestory?"

Several hands went up, then more, as everyone shared their excitement. Two young ladies had gone into a Hindu temple and spoke with the priest. He did not say yes at the end of the Lifestory, but he was very happy to hear what Jesus had done for him. He begged them to come back again to tell him more.

Two of the students were still out, and I was getting concerned. Finally, we heard them at the gate. They had another man with them. For security reasons, I approached them first to find out who the third person was.

The man was the principal of a nearby high school. He had just been born again. He said he wanted to know more about the training, but his real question was whether the two new Lifestory tellers could return to the school to tell the Lifestory to his five instructors and ultimately to the entire student body of two hundred.

We quickly sent them off with a short prayer, wishing them the best. The rest of the group continued sharing their testimonies about their experiences. It was very uplifting for them and surely gave them a sense of accomplishment. Over two hundred people had been approached by this group in less than an hour. By the end of the day, fourteen people had prayed to receive the Lord as their personal savior!

Two days later we took the group to a local pizza parlor for a treat. It was one of only two pizza places in the city. We received permission from the management to tell our server the Lifestory. There are five parts to the Lifestory, and a different person told each part. I got to be the one who prayed with him. Together we led the server to Jesus as a group.

Hand Motions

We sought the Lord amid increasing challenges as the lifestory movement continued expanding into new language groups. How could our master lifestory tellers (MLSTs) best communicate the lifestory across language barriers as they seek to start movements in new places?

God gave us a simple but profound solution with much wider benefits and we developed hand motions to accompany the lifestory.[5]

These gestures proved a great help to the lifestory movement in several ways. Gestures included the following: Gain and hold the listener's attention for the lifestory. Increase the listener's retention and understanding of the lifestory. Help lifestory tellers learn, rehearse, and tell the story. They also give a silent way for a partner to offer a reminder of what is next, just in case they are stalled while telling the story.

In this area there a multiple languages in service and the Hand motions help during the training by assisting people who are learning the story, or teaching it to someone who is basically trying to learn or teach across a language difference. Spreading the lifestory and winning souls in spite of a language difference is always a challenge. Hand motions help a lot.

---

[5] See the training tab at LifestoryTellers.net for a video showing the gestures.

ROLE OF OUTSIDERS

Later we had another training for believers like ourselves from outside the country. They wanted to try a different strategy from what we were pursuing. Instead of training local believers to tell the lifestory, they wanted to be the ones telling the lifestory to everyone.

We felt this would accomplish very little, but they wanted to try. As far as we know, this produced very little fruit.

Our experience suggests that those from outside the country who want to encourage a movement should seek to be the servant to those within the country, especially the local leaders they have led to the Lord with the Lifestory.

Local Leadership

Development of a movement requires the development of local leaders. We found that leaders in any new location develop in these stages:

tellers
teachers
teachers of teachers
district organizers

As each movement grows, additional levels of leadership develop beyond this basic structure. Master Lifestory teachers then strengthen each local movement, while Master Lifestory Teacherss, or Master Life Story Tellers are trained to start new lifestory movements in new places.

Training with Gulzar

Coach told us a group from the valley would be arriving for training as Lifestory tellers. As we were getting ready, I heard a rattle at the gate. Looking to the street, I saw a car totally covered in dust. The front windshield streaked from the wiper. The little car looked as if it had barely accomplished a hard journey, and four very large men still sat inside.

I called Coach and asked, "Could they be here already?" When he told me yes, I asked him to hurry over because I didn't speak their language. He assured me he was nearly there. *Thank you, God!*

I motioned for the driver to pull into the driveway. He twisted the little steering wheel, raced the little motor, and lurched a bit, then in they came. I noticed a lot about the little car that day. The tires were nearly bald, and the gas tank was totally empty. These men had more heart than they had hardware.

We were drawn to this bunch of guys. They were so happy. I wondered if they had no problems. Maybe they were overjoyed because they had made the long journey in one piece. We later found out that Jesus was the source of their joy. We liked that, and we loved Gulzar and his group of friends.

Gulzar was a large person with a broad, happy smile. Each time he greeted me and each time he bid me farewell, he gave me a huge hug. It was like hugging a grizzly bear.

The Lifestory mentions Jesus drawing all men to Himself. Up to this point, we used a gesture in which a Lifestory teller reaches straight out, then draws their hands back to themselves.

Coach was using that hand motion during the training, but as he did, Gulzar rose to his feet and exclaimed, "No, no! Like this!" And he stretched his great arms out like Jesus on the cross, then drew them back like he was hugging someone.

"Like this!" Gulzar repeated. That day we adopted Gulzar's way of showing Jesus—with open arms drawing all men to Himself.

We had two Gulzars in the Lifestory teams at that time. This was the one I knew personally. I was told the other Gulzar was much the same person. Both were hefty, happy, good men, each with a wife and children. Both, with a third person we knew well, are together with Jesus now.

Each was taken from their families by men who, as Jesus said on the cross, "Knew not what they were doing." Each left us too soon. Please keep their widows and orphans in your heart and prayers. We can never prepare for such things to happen, and no human wisdom can heal our hearts. Our healing must come from God.

LEARNING FROM THE MOVEMENT

We consider it another milestone when strategy emerges from within a movement itself. Their wise counsel tends to point us toward what Jesus would have us do.

The number of those new to trusting in Jesus was growing rapidly in proportion to the number of trained Lifestory tellers, so we held a strategy meeting of the most active and successful Lifestory tellers. We took a simple approach: Aim high and brace for expansion. The group set a goal of doubling the number of Lifestory tellers.

One thing we had learned: Don't look for a movement maker in the mirror. It takes more of God's effort and patience to move us into action who have known Jesus and yet have practiced inactivity. Our mouths have acidic opposition working against inviting people to follow Jesus. It is not impossible, but it appears that the first love effect is more exciting. People who are new in the faith look upward and thrilled with Jesus sometimes more than us and our friends who are comfortable believers. It appears to take something like a second calling for those who don't have a passion for inviting others to follow Jesus. That passion is not likely to appear suddenly. Although once it occurs in us it is monumental and older slaves of the Lord who come out of an older branch have the same sweet savor as the new.

In Mark 2, Jesus was sharing in Galilee after casting out demons and healing the sick. A group of people could not get close to Him with their friend. In desperation, they tore off the roof and lowered their friend down inside the packed building. Look at the results in Mark 2:10-12: "But that you may know that the Son of Man has power on earth to forgive sins"-He said to the paralytic, 11 "I say to you, arise, take up your bed, and go to your house."12 Immediately he arose, took up the bed, and went out in the presence of them all, so that all were amazed and glorified God saying, "We never saw anything like this!"

To start a movement, we must have a sense of urgency about offering everyone something they need right now, with a way to deliver it on demand. This "something" is readily available to all who believe—the blessing of God in Jesus. The critical factor is our sense of urgency about inviting others to follow Him.

What I *can* do toward starting a movement is seek out those who need Jesus the most. Once the experience Jesus they are best prepared to give their all to follow Jesus. Are they not the ones God will use to build a movement? Call the desperate and downtrodden, just as Jesus did in 1 Corinthians 1:27: "But God has chosen the foolish things of the world to put to shame the wise, and God has chosen the weak things of the world to put to shame the things which are mighty."

Better yet, we try not to predict who will lead a movement or who might welcome salvation. Limiting our witness by prejudging others implies we have a right to choose. Our role in following Jesus is inviting everyone to follow Him and trust the Lord of the harvest to raise up the laborers He chooses.

The best way to find people with the right sense of urgency is to tell everyone about Jesus as fast as we can, then guide those who respond to follow Him. We will see a movement when we find those to whom God gives this sense of urgency. We guide them to hear and follow Jesus and then we encourage them, but stay out of their way.

The lifestory leaders at our strategy meeting came to clear agreement regarding our next steps. They identified these problems and their solutions under the Lord's direction in accordance with scripture:

Problem One: People were having to travel too far to receive training, slowing the movement.

Solution: Train more Lifestory teachers in each area to teach those new to trusting Jesus how to tell the Lifestory. Local Lifestory Teachers bring multiplication and growth to an area.

Problem Two: If the community does not swiftly and widely

understand that the Lifestory is bringing God's blessing of eternal life in Jesus, they may get the wrong idea that the Lifestory is seeking to change their religion.[6]

Solution: Set high goals, with standardized training to achieve those goals.

This strategy team developed these 2011 and 2012 goals:

Train four master teachers—three for the Kashmir Valley area and one to assist in the Jammu area.

Produce a training manual to standardize the training.

Assist the widows.
Memorize scripture.

When this meeting was over, Messenger D asked for prayer, so we gathered around him. He was crying from severe pain in his head, so some laid their hands on him as we prayed. I did not want to let him leave, but his friends insisted they would make sure he was cared for. My heart was heavy for him, and we kept praying after he left.

---

[6] Religions frequently unite communities in a shared understanding of what *people* have to do to be right with God. Such communities are threatened when some in the community embrace another religion. The Lifestory tells how God makes us right with Him through faith in Jesus, not a change of religion, but a change of relationship.

Next Steps for Everyone

From this meeting it was proclaimed that the Lifestory movement model is simple:

Tell everyone the Lifestory.

Invite all who say yes to become a Lifestory teller and join a team.

Invite all Lifestory tellers to mature as Lifestory teachers.

Invite all Lifestory tellers to pursue one hundred yeses. This qualifies them to apply for training to become a Master Lifestory Teacher or a Master lifestory Teller.

Lifestory movements rely on the scriptures and the Holy Spirit to lead each telling of the lifestory. Standardized lifestory training from master teachers helps to give confidence to those learning to tell the Lifestory.

As God gives each lifestory teller fruit, they rely on what they learned from the Bible about Jesus Christ and the Holy Spirit. All the while training those who trust in Jesus to also tell the lifestory. And as these new lifestory tellers mature, each is encouraged to also attend a formal training with a master teacher.

As each movement grows, we aim for consistency in training new lifestory tellers through an authority structure of recognized leaders, teachers of teachers, and master teachers. We also cultivate MLSTs to carry the Lifestory into new areas.

Obtaining one hundred yeses is the prerequisite to apply for training to become a master lifestory teacher or a MLST. This is similar to the common requirement to earn a bachelor's degree before applying for a master's degree. After achieving this milestone of one hundred yeses, those aspiring for these master roles must then apply for master training and be recommended by a team leader, a MLST, or a master lifestory teacher.

Training to become a master lifestory teacher or a master lifestory teller includes:

1. Participating in a lifestory team.
2. Setting a goal for telling the Lifestory a certain number of times per day for the next three months and sharing that goal with someone.
3. Assisting in two Lifestory teller trainings led by a master teacher.
4. Setting a date to teach a Lifestory-teller training in the next year and communicating that date to a master teller or MLST

Why One Hundred Yeses?

Like a bachelor's degree in academia, obtaining one hundred yeses provides a strong foundation of insight and experience for training as a master teacher or an MLST.

When a person has followed Jesus in telling the Lifestory to obtain one hundred yeses, nearly all their why and how questions will have already been answered. They will likely have learned to multiply by training others whose own efforts contributed to their hundred yeses. And they will have developed a variety of ways to handle different objections and distractions.

The most fruitful early Lifestory tellers foresaw that requiring one hundred yeses before one could apply for training to mastery would provide a shared experience base to explore more advanced issues and help teachers focus on those most committed to fruitfulness.

The hundred yeses requirement also facilitates team formation by giving Lifestory tellers a goal in working together. Teams provide each member with mutual encouragement and prayer. Teams also may collaborate in sharing yeses—when the whole team of not more than three people averages one hundred yeses, every member of the team is credited with one hundred yeses. This works particularly well in remote locations where travel is difficult, or with handicapped tellers.

Out of the Depth Comes Life

The Tawi River flows through the center of Jammu. On the south bank, where the river bends back to the West, there is a Hindu temple. It is distinguished by a high pointed tower and a cement platform that goes right out to the water. The temple is a well known tourist attraction. Many Hindu people travel there to enjoy relaxation and refreshment.

The water recedes during the summer, and the hot weather entices people into the river for a cooling dip. Sometimes the swimmers drift near the temple, where the water is much deeper and cooler. Unfortunately, the current has an undercut, creating a hazardous undertow well known to the locals.

One day Coach was in the area. He left his fifteen-year-old son, who was not a strong swimmer, to wade downstream, where the water was shallow, while he took a towel and walked upstream to the temple foundation. Coach was an accomplished swimmer, so the undertow was not a problem for him. He enjoyed a cool swim around the foundation area; then he dried off and began his walk down the river to his son.

At the same time, two couples were taking an evening stroll beside the river, enjoying the cooling breeze that arose at the end of the day.

The stones along the riverbank were quite large, and in some places one must step from stone to stone in the middle of the path. As Coach reached that point, he glanced down into the river. To his surprise, he saw a white human hand reaching upward from the dark water. He immediately plunged in to help. As he came out of the water, he shouted to the couples down the river, "Come, help!"

He then noticed that one of the four was missing. The strollers saw the lady lying draped over the stones and rushed to her side.

Soon she was gasping for air. Her husband was beside himself. He had been in animated conversation with the other couple and had not noticed his wife's absence when she slipped and fell off one of the rounded stones.

Coach helped them to a more comfortable area and was smothered with praise and thanks by the husband. "Who are you?" he asked. "You saved my wife. You have done a very great thing. What can I do for you? I will do anything you want. I am so grateful to you. Please permit me to compensate you in some way for what you have done."

Coach turned to him and said, "I don't want any payment, but I would like to tell you a short story."

"Yes, of course! My name is Raj Kumar. I don't ever want to be a stranger to you from now on. Please tell us your story."

Coach told the Lifestory to the two couples. All four of them gave their whole hearts to Jesus. They were continually thanking both Coach and the Lord for saving Mrs. Kumar. Raj wrote down Coach's name and address so they could keep in touch.

It turned out Raj Kumar lived in Jaipur, known as the Pink City. He was well-to-do and is now an avid supporter of Lifestory movements. One month after his wife's near drowning, he returned to Jammu to take the Lifestory tellers training. He then started telling the Lifestory and reading the Bible. In one year. he accumulated three hundred committed believers. All were organized into their personal teams.

Coach planned a teacher training for the teachers of Jaipur. Raj Kumar continues to tell others about Jesus. By now, his fruit in the Jaipur area has expanded to include five major teams with mixed ethnic backgrounds. He announced to coach that there were now 300 teams.

M. Awan

M. Awan was introduced earlier in the chapter about the motorcade. After that beginning M. Awan was continuing to do great things. Coach had given him a hundred or so copies of the Lifestory in Urdu. He then organized a meeting with his political party, and fifty people attended. Handing each person a copy of the Lifestory, he asked everyone to follow along as he read the Lifestory out loud. He then asked them to raise their hands if they would say yes to trusting the Lord Jesus to save them. Without any hesitation, they all came to Jesus that night.

M. Awan and I had a short meeting one day. We could feel the Lord's presence there with us. We are brothers and friends for life. A few years later, he and an important official came to town. We met in a secure location. As he gave me a big hug, the first words out of his mouth were, "My favorite book is Ephesians." It is rare to find a person who makes people feel joyful just by being around them. He caused us to feel that way with what seemed like little effort.

The Lifestory tellers of Kashmir consider M. Awan most wise. They affectionately call him the problem-solver. The name fits him; he is a genius at getting people on the right side of peace and stability.

For instance, there was a time when he was in a political race for a certain district. It is common for these things to be very competitive, and rivals are sometimes mortal enemies. M. Awan had finished his campaign speech in one area and decided to visit another town where someone he knew was also campaigning. That person was sharing Jesus with a different ethnic group that was not friendly with Muslims, but M. Awan considered the man to be his friend, so he joined the crowd and listened to the speech with visible interest.

The man finished his speech, then waded into the crowd to shake hands with his followers. He easily spotted M. Awan and came over to him, asking: "What are you doing here?"

Knowing M. Awan was the senior politician in the state, the man immediately offered him half of the district, even though he appeared somewhat reluctant as he made the gesture. But M. Awan replied, "I came here because I am your friend, and I wanted to see you. Hello, my friend! I have a short story. Would you like to hear it?"

The politician was baffled, but he agreed to listen to the story. Five minutes later, M. Awan came to the part in which the man could answer yes or no to trusting Jesus to save him. The man said no. He added, "I would say yes to this because it is good, but if I do I will lose all my followers and all my supporters."

M. Awan lovingly reproved him. "Dear friend, this may be true. But if you don't have Jesus, you don't have anything."

A moment later, the man replied, "Okay, then I take Jesus."

M. Awan gave him a bear hug, and they laughed together. "Dear friend," M. Awan said, "I will give you my supporters, and I will come and work for you."

The man replied, "No, I will give you mine, and I will come and work for you!"

After a vigorous discussion, they both decided to go on doing what they do as politicians, but they would both lift Jesus up to all their people.

There have been many crises in the state of Kashmir. In all circumstances, Brother Awan guides the Lifestory tellers with wisdom and patience. He is kindhearted, and his patience encourages us to wait when necessary. This helps us keep from making grave mistakes.

News Flash for Today

I call my partner Coach for security reasons. I have similarly masked the political positions and names of others in this book.

As I write this in early 2018, there has been a major development.

I called Coach early one morning. After answering, he said, "Excuse me, someone is at the gate. I'll be right back." He returned in less than a minute and quickly informed me that a vehicle had arrived. The driver said that one of our Lifestory friends, a well-known community leader, was requesting Coach's immediate presence.

Coach needed to dress and shave, so I hung up and said a prayer for him. It was late evening before I heard from him again. I called him just as he arrived home. He told me he was very nervous because of the way the official had required his immediate attention. Telling him I also felt that way, I asked him what happened.

Upon arrival at the official's house, Coach saw five men in serious discussion. Among them were the well-known community leader and several diplomats. Coach and his team had trained one of these men, and Coach wondered if that man's sharing had caused problems.

Coach was relieved to learn they were gathered to finalize the engagement of the official's son and the daughter of one of the other men. The families of both the groom and the bride were avid Lifestory tellers. Many guests were about to arrive for the party, including five prominent Muslim clerics and numerous important witnesses to the event. The leader said that Coach would have the honor of presenting the Lifestory to the guests.

These leaders made history by breaking tradition concerning the dowry, giving relief to others planning marriages in the area. Telling the Lifestory that day resulted in fifty-two of the guests saying yes to Jesus and eternal life.

Geographic Expansion

Soon the Lifestory tellers were itching to take the good news to distant parts, even where outsiders were not welcome.

HIGHER CALLING IN A HIGH PLACE

Shah and Rakis are leaders in Ladakh[7] who are raising up skilled Lifestory tellers. Shah was one of the first people to take the Lifestory training with us (see chapters 28 and 29). He wasted no time in becoming an admired and productive fisher of men. Both he and Rakis are full of grace and knowledge, and they were essential in leading the team through the harsh winter.

Shah set his sights high. He took Rakis and four other men—Mohideen, Mahmuda, Rakesh, and Samad, along with one woman, Gazelle—with him to Kargil. Kargil is one of the highest cities in the world and the second-largest town in Ladakh. Shah personally watched over Gazelle, who became a door to salvation for the women of the region.

The snow was still receding when the team arrived in Kargil.

---

[7] Ladakh is a region in the central and eastern part of Jammu-Kashmir.

They shared the Lifestory as they made arrangements to rent a house. By the time they moved in, their team had grown through sharing the Lifestory to over thirty Lifestory tellers. All of them were multilingual and capable of sharing the Lifestory cross culturally. There would be a good harvest.

Many in that area were Buddhist. At the first home they visited, an older couple took them in, fed them well, and gave them rest. Their son, Shangi, liked the Lifestory so much he became an avid follower of Jesus as his personal savior. Shangi's father is a Buddhist priest. Now this priest and his wife love Jesus. Shangi knew everyone in Kargil and where everything was. He quickly became the team's go-to person.

Under Shangi's direction, the team spread out to tell the Lifestory among the Buddhist population of Kargil. They then gathered to share their results. The report was simple: Everyone contacted said yes to following Jesus! Lifestory-teller training and scripture sharing would soon begin. This was a great start.

The team was well cared for by Shangi's family, and their home became a haven. They will share a joyful destiny forever.

JON SMITH

Another of the first followers of Jesus there was Paljor. He is a gift and a giver, with godly insight to see the good in people and to connect them to Jesus and walk beside them with the Word of God. All these people gather now in the upper Himalayas to begin another chapter in their lives with Jesus.

SHOE ISSUE SOLVED

Several of the men were eager to visit a town where they had quite a few relatives waiting to see them. While this town sits over eleven thousand feet, the surrounding peaks reach fifteen to seventeen thousand feet. It takes time to learn how to breathe again when one reaches these elevations.

Most of the population is Shia,[8] originally from the area around Iran and Iraq. The team arrived and began to search for relatives. They found a few right way, including some they had never met. All were glad to see them and to catch up on family news.

But the people of this town did not seem to be as open to the Lifestory as those back in Kargil. We realized something was wrong when the town elders approached the teachers and demanded they stop teaching the Lifestory. All those connected to the situation considered this to be very serious.

The Shia are very concerned that no one ever profane a prophet. During the training, we were introducing a simple memory system to help people remember the five parts of the Lifestory. The second part of the Lifestory is remembered by thinking of a pair of shoes. Honorable Adam is one shoe, and Eve is the other. But to the Shia, it was offensive to disgrace the prophet Adam by putting his name on a shoe. Something had to be done.

The Lifestory tellers contacted the team leaders and Coach. They even gave me a call. The best advice was from the teams. They suggested all of us solemnly pray for guidance from the Lord. We prayed, and God gave them an answer.

---

[8] One of two main branches of Islam, Shia reject the first three Sunni caliphs and regard Ali—the fourth caliph—as Muhammad's first true successor.

The issue was a misunderstanding, and we humbly apologized for not making it clear that Honorable Adam and Eve were a pair, just like shoes are a pair. Individual shoes are not named, only the pair together. As a result, we corrected this in all our trainings.

The next part of the team's agenda was difficult, and they needed to organize a small army of supporters to accomplish their plan. But by then God had more than a hundred people in the area who had become Lifestory tellers following Jesus as their savior.

Above this town was an even higher village, with nothing else that high but yak herders. The Lifestory tellers did not have to ask the Lord if they should go; they felt the Lord had already made it clear.

Commodities were so scarce in this upper village that a modest thing like a bucket of water cost more than two hundred Indian rupees, which totaled more than two days' wages. Winters at this altitude were harsh. For added insulation, permanent dwellings were built partially below ground level. Both animals and humans have to stay inside to survive the cold. Staying at these elevations could have various harmful effects on the visiting team, such as aging their skin, damaging their lungs, and freezing body parts.

The team would need supplies before moving to this area, and they would have to adjust to a new way of life to survive the coming winter.

For the most part, things went well. But supplies got very low, and Rakeesh had to evacuate because of frostbite. He lost a toe and was warned not to come back, because now his feet would always be susceptible to freezing. This did not deter him from returning, however, as he had become highly interested in a certain somebody who lived there! He continues to share the Lord in that area.

Hardships were plenty, but the rewards were like precious diamonds. The people living there were so grateful that someone would bring them the good news. The sparkle of new life came into the eyes of many who had never dared to dream that God included them in His family through His precious word.

With help from Jesus, and through our prayers, the team survived the winter. They had asked us to pray that they will have one meal a day. Let every bite we eat remind us to pray for their provision and that their labor in Jesus will result in many being saved.

BROTHER SHAH THE PEACEMAKER

In another region, military conflict between warring governments meant a city on one side of a river was being frequently shelled from the opposite side. The cannons had taken their toll, and many had left the area. The city had become a ghost town, with nearly every shop closed, schools abandoned, and empty shells everywhere.

Brother Shah was trying to tell the Lifestory to those remaining in the town, but the artillery barrage made it difficult.

Many on both sides of the river were friends and relatives, even though they were under different governments, and Shah happened to know Mr. A, the officer in charge of the artillery.

One night Shah elected to cross the bridge to pay a visit to Mr. A.

Once Shah crossed the bridge, it was not difficult to find his friend. After making his request to the guard, only a few minutes passed before they were face-to-face.

Mr. A invited Shah to his quarters. They exchanged greetings, but little was said about the past or about others they both knew. Mr. A asked, "What are you doing here?"

Shah was quick to answer. "I have come with a Lifestory team to help people who are in need."

"What are you doing to help?"

"First we offer to tell the Lifestory. Even if they are not interested, we show we care by helping in any way we can. It is difficult, as people are very upset because of the shelling."

"How many are there with you?" he asked.

Shah replied, "There are only seven, but three widows have joined us to clean up the schools."

"Why are you cleaning up the schools?" Shaw said:"We do this to get their attention so they will listen to the story,"

The official replied: "Okay, Shah, tell me about this story. Why is it so important?"

"It is short. Perhaps you would like to hear it yourself?"

The official declared, "You must tell me the story now."

Shah obeyed the command and told the officer the Lifestory. After hearing the Lifestory, the officer asked, "Is this true, my friend?"

"Yes, it is true. Jesus loves you!"

A moment passed before the officer sincerely replied, "Since this is true, I say yes to trusting Jesus to save me."

Both men were happy that God had interrupted life as they knew it to bring a new beginning to the officer.

Mr. A asked more questions about the status and intents of the people on the other side. Shah told him they were all commoners who had no hostility. Most were poor and only trying to make it through the winter. He assured him there were only local people on the other side. They said a friendly goodbye, and Shah left to return to the other side.

In the days following, something changed. The soldier could not change his orders from headquarters, but the shelling came later in the afternoon, and the targets were now open fields instead of structures. Every time a shell was launched, the gun crews would pray and aim far away from civilian areas. Shah made frequent visits across the bridge, as he taught the officer to become a Lifestory teller.

The dear women on the Lifestory team worked hard to clear the rubble around the school and sweep out the building. Soon one section was ready for students, and classes could begin. They stayed on to help get things back to normal. Some elementary students came back, and the Lifestory team ladies taught them for a while. Life had improved because the officer in charge was now under God's command.

The residents noticed the great changes that were occurring. Their prayers for peace were beginning to bear fruit. As a result, they were open to hearing the Lifestory, and many turned their hearts to Jesus.

RETREAT TO VICTORY

Thanks to God, we had a direct answer to prayer when one of our training teams escaped an area of great trouble. Shah and the team canceled their training in Shopian,[9] making a fast exit on foot as the area erupted into gunfire, shouting, and high-velocity stone slinging. All roads were blocked, and a curfew would surely be imposed.

The team walked single file along the main roads and paths that led from village to village. They traveled somewhat separated, listening carefully for signs of trouble before entering each village along the way. By nightfall they had traveled nearly thirty miles and were just one village from home.

But the team realized this last village was too quiet, and the homes appeared dark, vacant, and locked. They wanted to press on as quickly as possible, but they felt an urgent sense they should proceed cautiously.

Suddenly they spotted a dim light in the back of a butcher shop. Since some butchers are willing to sell after hours, Shah called out, and a large burly man appeared.

"Could we come in for the night?" Shah asked.

The butcher replied pleasantly, "Please come in and have some food with us." Four Lifestory team members, including one lady, sat together in the dim light and enjoyed a nice meal with the butcher and his family. Everything seemed to be going fine.

Then the butcher rose to speak, but he seemed to be stumbling over his words. "I, uh, would like to, uh, share something with you. Years ago this came to me from a friend. I have not told this to anyone else. But since you are here, I feel it is okay. It is a story."

---

[9] Shopian is an ancient town of around twelve thousand inhabitants, thirty-three miles from Srinagar.

As the butcher continued, the team recognized the story as their own Lifestory and began to chuckle, amazed at God's timing and provision. With great joy, they heard the butcher relate how—five years earlier—Messenger D had told the Lifestory to this very butcher. But under persecution, the local followers of Jesus had succumbed to fear, and few were telling the Lifestory.

Now, guided by divine providence, Shah and the team had come to this very village and met this same butcher, giving the local followers of Jesus a second chance to learn to expressively tell the Lifestory. The team arranged to return and hold a training session for them.

M. Awan and the Governor

In those days, M. Awan was privileged to visit the governor. First on his agenda was finding a private moment when M. Awan could tell the Lifestory. Sure enough, after dinner they were enjoying a cup of tea together when M. Awan asked the governor if he wanted to hear a short story. The governor told him to go ahead.

M. Awan told him the Lifestory. When he was finished, he noticed a slight smile on the governor's face. He was quiet for a moment. M. Awan asked him again, "Would you say yes or no to trusting Jesus?" M. Awan later reported, "I can tell you only this: his answer was good!"

Dinner Surprise

One evening M. Awan was at home sharing some time with his Lifestory team. They had finished their Bible study and were relaxing over a meal together. M. Awan was in the open area at the back of the house. It was a good place for a large person and his many friends to sit back and enjoy their fellowship.

With his plate in his lap, M. Awan reclined in his casual white tunic while his lovely wife and daughter served the meal. The garden around about them was lush with beautiful ferns and blooming flowers.

Suddenly a plate crashed onto the marble floor, and several shouted and jumped to their feet. Something long, black, and sinuous flashed across the floor. Many bolted in the opposite direction, while the snake anxiously searched for a safe exit from the garden.

The reptile swiftly crossed the garden and chose a hiding spot under the white tent of fabric covering M. Awan's legs. He quickly tried to rise and dislodge the creature, but it was too late. The snake had fastened its jaws onto his thigh.

Others tried to help, but the snake was long, and efforts to remove it were ineffective. Finally, one of the men grasped the head and squeezed, forcing the mouth open. Blood was now pouring from the wound. M. Awan's white tunic was crimson from waist to floor. Working quickly, the men hurried to get him into the car, then raced to the hospital. A long black snake in this part of the country usually meant one thing: king cobra! But in the rush to get M. Awan to the hospital, the snake had been left behind. This meant the doctor could not administer antivenom, because he could not identify with certainty the type of snake.

Later that night we still had no word from the hospital. We

prayed. Early the next morning we learned that M. Awan was still alive.

The medical team kept M. Awan overnight for observation and to run additional tests. It would be difficult to bring the snake to the hospital because of its huge size. Besides, in Jammu it is against Hindu law to harm the snake. Perhaps this law has something to do with this city's distinction as the poisonous snakebite capital of the world.

During the night M. Awan showed no negative symptoms except for bruising from the vicious bite. They brought him home the next day, and we all breathed a sigh of relief for M. Awan's recovery and safe return. They also searched for the snake and found it dead.

JON SMITH

THE POSWAL

The Poswal are a shepherd clan found in Afghanistan, Pakistan, and India. They are fiercely independent, with a distinct way of dealing with the world. With much confidence, they question every new idea. It's a momentous event to offend someone. One member of this clan heard the Lifestory from M. Awan. Here is Yasur's response:

Last year my father and I visited the world famous *Jhiri* mela[10] in Jammu. We met M. Awan, who is my father's friend. He told my father a story.

We were in a tea stall, and I was also listening, but I had to stop when I heard we have broken our relationship with God. I was unable to hear more, because it was horrifying to me.

I was lost mentally! In my heart, I was thinking, *How can one restore this relationship?* I returned home and met with religious persons and asked the question, "How can we restore our broken relationship with God?" I read many religious books in search of an answer, but I failed. My life became disturbed due to a lack of certainty about God's forgiveness.

At last I decided to meet Uncle Awan privately. I made the arrangement and met with him. It was six months after my great disturbance. He was at Lakhimpur during his political trip to the area. We met, he hugged me, and whispered in my ear that he knew I would come for this. I could tell he was very busy dealing with lots of people, but no matter. He took time to meet me separately in a private corner of the park.

---

[10] An annual fair held in Jammu during October through November, it honors the legend of a farmer named Baba Jitto, who committed suicide after he was cheated by the feudal landowner of the area. The Jhiri Mela signifies the honesty, innocence, humility, courage, culture, and truthfulness of a farmer.

There he told me the Lifestory without any stops. When he asked me yes or no, I could not speak, because inside I was going through a long journey of soul-searching. In a moment of great power, I opened my mouth, and I said yes to Jesus! Suddenly everything stopped, and there was no noise to be heard. Even the people were quiet. I did not sense anything in the world around me, but I felt a great peace in my entire being. Jesus, His sweet loving name, was covering me all over!

The Lifestory tellers thank Yasur for this testimony. It will bring peace to many.

The Poswal are a special gift from God, called by Him to care for their region. The first training in their area was a dream come true for M. Awan. It was by his encouragement and counsel that others in the state were moved to help this important group find peace with God through the Lord Jesus.

TRAINING AT MANSAR LAKE

Ahamad has been living an abundant life since following Jesus and telling the Lifestory. One day he was counting it a privilege to travel with the other Lifestory tellers to hold a training for the Poswal.

The event would be held in the area surrounding Mansar Lake, a popular excursion destination and holy site—a one-hour drive into the mountains of central Kashmir. The road traverses the side of a ridge, offering a panoramic view of the villages and farms on the valley floor below.

The residents of the area are a diverse group. Because the Poswal are well known and have great influence, the Lifestory tellers felt it necessary to go and lead some among them to follow Jesus. It would be a great step forward for everyone to see many Poswal come to trust Christ as the way of eternal Life.

The travelers hardly noticed the rough road. They descended into the lake area, then stopped in a restaurant parking lot.

It was easy to spot the men waiting to accompany the travelers to the training site. The waiting men were dressed in white, with folded wool topis on their heads. Each had a smile and gave a warm greeting as they joined the others in the dusty car. Leaving the lake behind, they continued on for a few miles to the next village.

The next part of their journey would be on foot. The path was well marked, but it was rather steep. Thankfully, many trees shaded the trail.

A young man was riding a horse up the trail, with a friend seated behind him. The young man's father had given him the horse, and he was quite proud of it. The horse was spirited, sidestepping and tossing his head as if warning his rider he might break into a gallop at any moment.

They were truly a sight, these two young men on a white

horse, prancing up the trail. Ahamad later learned they, too, were candidates for the master teacher training. Others caught up to the visiting teachers as they hiked. By the time the teachers could see the first house in the village, nearly a dozen trainees were accompanying them on the trail. Another group was already there, waiting.

The house was well suited for the training, with a number of rooms that allowed for smaller groups. Outside several women were cooking maize roti and a vegetable stew on a chula—a native stove of hardened clay. Inside one of the more famous teachers, known as the Signpost, was already teaching the early group. The Poswal group accepted the training with grace and peace.

Weeks earlier a group of Lifestory tellers and teachers had come to train those who first trusted in Jesus in this area as Lifestory tellers. Their goal was to build up these new Lifestory tellers so that each of them would achieve the agreed upon one hundred yeses to qualify to apply for training to become a master teacher or master Lifestory teller (MLST) and then pursue such training. Ahamad was eager to meet everyone and explain the goal to the twenty-three new candidates. He would be overseeing this master teacher training.

To encourage fruitfulness and shorten the time for all to receive one hundred yeses, the leaders recommended that Lifestory tellers form teams of two or three to encourage and pray for one another. This way those who were more successful would assist those who were not. When these teams averaged more than one hundred yeses per team member, all team members were credited with one hundred yeses.

God has given us a great tool: "I have a short story. It takes five minutes. Would you like to hear it?"

We have seen many Lifestory movements begin and grow from this simple question. This question starts a conversation that quickly introduces Jesus and leads many toward hearing and following Him. The Lifestory rallies people, encouraging them to share the Gospel while keeping them focused on God's desire for everyone to be saved. God works through the Lifestory teller's dedication.

At this training, Ahamad saw the Lord's hand moving among the new trainees. Surely something great was unfolding—and it was God's blessing in Jesus for those who had been waiting so long in the darkness for His wonderful light.

Late that evening, as the fire was dying and Ahamad and his

friends were finishing their chai, a dark figure approached. To their surprise, it was a woman. She approached in all humility and asked, "Sir, could I try to become a Lifestory teller?"

Ahmad was surprised. "Of course. This will be okay, but first you will need to take the Lifestory-teller training. We will have to arrange it. The ladies' teams will come when you are ready."

Later the teachers discussed her request and agreed it would be just like the Lord to start a new movement among the women of the area.

M. Dard, door to door

M. Dard

Messenger D went to jail and shared the Lifestory, and brought freedom to five prisoners. M. Dard was one of those prisoners. He was so changed by his new life in Christ that the authorities commuted his sentence and released him.

The local Lifestory team assigned me to meet with M. Dard. Some were afraid of M. Dard's violent past. The leadership felt it would be good for everyone if they could hear my opinion of him. Messenger D made the arrangements, and we travelled to a pass high in the mountains between Jammu and Srinagar and met in a cabin in a secluded area just off the main road.

I followed the directions to the cabin, perched on a steep ravine. The back of the house overlooked a vast expanse of mountains, partially covered with timber and brush. I called out at the door and waited. I was very relieved to see Coach open the door and invite me in.

It was dark inside, and it took a while for my eyes to adjust. A group of men sat in a half circle facing me. Coach began to introduce each one. M. Dard was tall and graced with a pleasant smile, but a closer and more careful observance revealed something different about his lower left arm. It was a bit shocking at first that all the fingers of his left hand were missing. It was later explained to me that this was a result of his practice of making things that would destroy temples from other religions. No doubt it had something to do with his reputation as the most dangerous person in Kashmir.

Jon's first impression of M. Dard was that he was awesome. He said: "The more I got to know him, the more accurate I found this impression. M. Dard is one of the most tender hearted, generous individuals I have ever met. I can hardly imagine him to be any other way. His change is a huge reference to the power of Christ for changing people from darkness into light."

M. Dard's way of kindness has traveled through all areas of the Valley. Whenever the Lifestory tellers in his area have a gathering, they have his support. He sometimes gives a whole sheep, and more, to feed them at the event. M. Dard was broke when he was released from prison. He started with three sheep and a couple of goats someone gave him and he found ways to feed and multiply them. Soon his flocks numbered over three hundred.

M. Dard did the same with his Lifestory team. He has been a catalyst for networks and for increasing fellowship with other teams.

He was given one of the most difficult places to gather laborers for the harvest. Early in his ministry, he was trusted to help the highly dispersed people in Frozen Lake. It is one of the most rural areas. In some places, houses are miles apart.

This problem was overcome because God had a special plan for this man and the shepherd teams he leads. Within a short time, the number of Lifestory tellers under his care increased dramatically. The key was to network small groups into one purpose: to follow Jesus.

M. Dard's network came up with the idea for *gariki* masjid (house mosques). These have become worship centers and network hubs for further expansion. The number of Lifestory tellers in these networks is conservatively estimated at five thousand.

We have seen the Lord move highly effective groups like those of M. Dard into areas with serious problems. M. Dard put out a plan to the rest of the teams in North Kashmir—he asked them to pray that one of the Shepherd teams could go into an especially volatile area in Jammu-Kashmir. Not many are willing to venture there, let alone bring a message that might be controversial.

M. Dard took a group of five men and four women, all veteran Lifestory tellers, to a city along the border of Pakistan. There they began to tell the Lifestory. In one report, they had led twenty three to trust in Jesus. When phone service stopped, we prayed that the angels of God would camp around them and protect them.

The phones came back on, and we heard from M. Dard that they were okay, but they were staying indoors because of a curfew. The area had become a battleground between opposing military forces. We eventually learned that M. Dard was at the hospital there, suffering from a stomach illness. He recovered, and with the others and he had a very successful time establishing the Lifestory movement in that area.

MESSENGER D STILL ACTIVE

A group of eight Lifestory leaders were meeting with Messenger D. They had been together for several days and were praying all night. Much of the prayer was for Coach and the future of the Lifestory movement.

They did not know that Coach's daughters were suffering from a terrible affliction, yet they proclaimed that one of his daughters was going to be healed.

There was also a great need to pray for Messenger D because his wife had asked for a divorce. Details were not provided, but all the teams were asked to pray. The Lifestory tellers agreed that Jesus would overcome this if we prayed.

Things didn't get any better for Messenger D. Still, he persisted in telling the Lifestory. Many locals thought he should stop. We think some were jealous because of his popularity, while others were angry because they thought him a blasphemer.

A constable set up a sting for Messenger D in a local hotel. Two men posing as truck drivers were sent into a hotel, and they asked to see the man with the great story. Messenger D was asked to talk with them. As he reached the halfway point of the Lifestory, the police came through the door and arrested him. The two men swore he had blasphemed against the temple, then stood by their lying testimony. Messenger D was sentenced and sent to jail.

Out of fear, no one would represent Messenger D or lend him money for bail. After he had suffered for three months in appalling conditions in the same jail that he had visited and brought deliverance to M. Dard., we collected enough money to help.

M. Awan was brave enough to take the funds to the authorities and beg for Messenger D's release. Wonderfully, they agreed.

But when M. Awan found him in the jail, Messenger D was just skin and bones, nearly naked, his body full of sores and too weak to walk. M. Awan took Messenger D straight to the hospital, where they kept him in emergency care for nearly a month. After his release, M. Awan brought Messenger D home and cared for him personally.

Later one night, Messenger D tried to go back to his own home. He was dreaming of a new place to share the good news. Jon called him and prayed with him. He said, "Praise the Lord, Brother."

Jon asked him to be careful because those who opposed him would continue to be a danger to him.

The teams agreed it was best that Jon stay away. This was *their* movement from God; Jon must be an outsider.

On June 22, 2012, Messenger D's lifeless body was found beside an irrigation ditch near the mosque in his hometown. He appeared to have been badly beaten. He was thirty-eight years old.

We remember from that nearly a year before his arrest Messenger D had been taken to face an inquisition. His accusers had been proved wrong; he had not blasphemed against Islam, and he was set free. This time they had stopped the dreamer, but not the dream.

The new place where Messenger D had been dreaming to tell the Lifestory, now has two Lifestory tellers in place and they are people that he trained. People are hearing the good news and coming to the Lord. The dreamer is in his own place now. He is in the arms of Jesus.

For years the police report stated he had been drunk and fell into a ditch. This report may have been compiled by the constable who set up the sting. The report has now been corrected by the police, and Messenger D's death is listed as a homicide. His death was a tragedy.

Messenger D was a good man who cared for his children. More than that, he was known by all the Lifestory tellers as a great witness for the Lord Jesus. He exalted the Lord and helped great numbers of men and women find salvation in Jesus.

For those who will more than consider becoming laborers for the harvest of Jesus Christ and will move to picking up the lifestory we have presented this and have shown how to use it like the people mentioned in this book have used it. We pray that all will let it come to their minds and hearts to follow the Lord Jesus into a life that is more than abundant. It is for those that we write this book. And even more it is for those who pick this up and go out and start a team and a movement. To you we will be a company of reborn people who will cheer you on and know how you feel in the great things that happen on this earth with you and Jesus, and the terrible things that He carefully shepherds you through. We are closer to you now because of our experience and because of Jesus.

VICTORY BEYOND DEATH

The Lifestory movement had suffered martyrdom of an important leader, but this would not slow the movement.

More Sharing of the Lifestory

A van with three Lifestory tellers was nearing the entrance of a tunnel. This tunnel connects greater India on one side to the valley of North Kashmir on the other. The tunnel is so long it would take the men nearly thirty minutes to drive to the other end.

After the tunnel they went down the winding road then came into the village they had called home for many years. But this time it was different. Inside their hearts was a burning treasure.

The Creator had called them to share this treasure with others. It was the first time for them to tell the Lifestory at home, and there was a lot at stake. What if their friends rejected the Lifestory?

They remembered how Jesus had helped them in the past and how he had come into their hearts. They were partnering with the living God, and they would obey his command to go and catch men.

They walked together through the village, stone fences lining their path on either side. Coming to the house of a friend, they said, "Let us start here. *Bismillah-ir-Rahkman-ir-Rahim.* We will start all things with God." So they started sharing the very story that brought them to the saviour. One at a time, each of these brothers in the Spirit shared the truth and drew their friends and family into the pure love of God.

The day was finished, and darkness had fallen. Tea was served, and friends and family blessed each other. Once the evening concluded, they embraced and departed.

Sheik M. turned to Abdu and Alfaz. "We must tell Coach how God has blessed us greatly and answered our prayers this day." Right then their cell phone rang. It was Coach, eager to hear the good news about their day of sharing.

"It is a great day," they said. "All our friends love us more than ever. Today we told the Lifestory to many, and forty-nine of our old friends said yes to Jesus. God is truly great!"

Coach was thrilled to hear the good news. He returned their blessings and praised them for their efforts.

SHARING IN DELHI CLINIC

Back in chapter 60, we learned Coach's daughter was suffering from a terrible affliction. The Lifestory tellers were unaware of this, yet during a time of prayer they heard from the Lord that she would be healed.

On this day, Coach brought his daughter to a clinic in Delhi for the second of three treatments required that month. After they came inside together, she was placed in a room by herself for an infusion, while Coach stayed in the waiting room.

A man came with his wife and daughter through the waiting room door. The daughter's face was covered with sores, and her father was sobbing inconsolably. Coach began a conversation, hoping to comfort him. He found out that the family was from Kanpur, in Utter Pradesh, about sixty miles east of Delhi.

Coach told the father that it was nice to meet him, then he said, "I have a short five minute story that will help you feel better." The parents replied, "Please tell us." The man's daughter was lying on a chair and seemed to be unconscious.

Coach got to the part in the opening of the Lifestory that tells how Jesus took all our sins to the grave and paid for them. Suddenly, the girl sat up and braced herself with her arms. "Did you say He took all our sins to the grave and paid for them?" Coach replied: "Yes."

Coach quickly finished telling the Lifestory; then he looked around and saw he had an audience. Everyone was watching him closely. Another couple had entered the waiting room and heard the Lifestory. Even the nurses and practitioners were peering out from behind the white curtains.

Coach addressed both couples and the daughter. "Will you look up to Jesus Christ right now and ask for forgiveness of sins and be saved, yes or no?" Everyone replied: " yes!"

The girl and her father wept for joy. Both couples prayed for forgiveness of their sins, asking Jesus to come into their lives and be their saviour. Each expressed gratitude for the Lifestory and for the new peace they had found in Jesus.

Coach also heard weeping from behind many of the curtains from both patients and doctors. Their tears confirmed that many had received a touch from Jesus.

Later Coach and his daughter returned to their home and shared with the family all that had happened. It was a lot to rejoice about, and it included the good news that the doctor's had confidence that Coach's daughter would get well again.

JAKTI CAMP EMERGENCY

Back in Jammu, Arjand and Ravi shared the Lord with their communities. Their previous work had been in the Jakti camp. This camp was providing emergency quarters for those in poverty.

Arjand and Ravi took responsibility for introducing the camp to the Lifestory. They called for other teams of Lifestory tellers to help them, and a campaign was started.

As they shared the Lifestory throughout the camp, they became acquainted with the people and noticed the great needs they had. They lacked food and other necessities in their meager homes. Many were in poor health and on the edge of starvation. Yet the people were very open to the Lord.

Bringing the Lifestory into the community revealed a vast and serious problem. Many families lacked hope of surviving the winter.

Arjand was keen to find the cause for the emergency. As he asked around, the people explained that outside assistance had been cut off. Of the twelve hundred people who came to trust the Lord on the first three days of the outreach, nearly everyone was suffering this same problem.

The Lifestory tellers made a decision to join the people in their suffering. They did this by beginning a complete fast, intending to fast and pray for the people of a suburb of Jammu called the Jakti camp until the crisis was over.

Then Arjand and other Lifestory leaders contacted those who had previously been providing assistance. They waited, but they received no response. Days went by. More teams of Lifestory tellers joined the struggle through a district-wide time of prayer and fasting. Outside of the Jammu district, other teams heard about the need and joined in prayer for their Lifestory brothers and the people of the Jakti camp.

Over the following week, the Lifestory leadership repeatedly contacted the offices of those who had been supplying assistance. One week of fasting and prayer went by. The situation was becoming dire. By this time, Lifestory teams in all parts of the state were aware of the situation. It became an important cause for all to rally around. Most of the Lifestory tellers were unable to share much in the way of food or finances due to their own limitations, but they joined in praying. Two more days went by as the cry of the people and the Lifestory tellers went up to the Lord.

Then one day more, and the Lord moved in the hearts of those who had been providing assistance. An announcement was made that sustenance would immediately be provided. Delivery points were set up, and the people were saved from starvation. The allotments for rice, flour, and sugar were doubled from what they had been before.

The cash stipends went from three thousand to seven thousand rupees per month for each family. Arjand's team, the people of Jakti camp, and the Lifestory tellers statewide were jumping for joy at what the Lord had done.

This answer to prayer made things better for the Lifestory tellers. They were welcomed with open arms into every home. Other communities heard of this and were eager to learn more about the teams who would come and share God's plan and pray for them. The Lifestory movement itself was gaining a good reputation.

Through the Flood, And through the Blood

Arjand and Ravi became servants of the Lord in difficult times. One season the rain came in torrents and did not let up. It just kept raining and raining.

Arjand and Ravi were training two Master Lifestoryteller candidates in a remote area. It was Asgat's and Alifaz's final training before they would be awarded master Lifestory teller status. Their master's thesis, so to speak, was to introduce every person in the village to Jesus.

The small village was on a slope; level ground was non-existent. Over a hundred souls called the perch above the canyon their home. The houses were built of wood and mortared stones. The two men had been there for almost a month. In the first two weeks, they found that getting a yes from people their age was simple. The first time they met the people there, they immediately told the Lifestory and most of the men their age came to Jesus Christ. The women and children came to Jesus next, along with a couple of older men.

Finally, there remained just two people between Asgat and Alifaz and their goal. If these two accepted the Lord, the men could depart for Kishtwar and start their life's work as MLSTs. They figured that these last two wouldn't be a big problem, because both were pleasant to be around and to talk to.

Haji was the grandfather of Sonja, and her sole support. Even though she was only fifteen years old, she had a lot of knowledge about spiritual things and the Koran. She tested the young men on everything they told her about the Lifestory. It seemed like every day she would have a new question about trusting Jesus as her savior. "How do I know God will really accept me?" she asked.

Alifaz tried to convince her that God loves everyone. He said, "God made you exactly as He wants you, so He will accept you."

Meanwhile, the rain was getting worse, and the two Lifestory tellers were getting nervous about their travel. Their teachers would arrive tomorrow, and they wished to have everything completed so they could be approved as MLSTs. Having prayed for an answer to their dilemma, they agreed to try something a bit daring.

Asgat had noticed that Sonja seemed more interested in Alifaz than in making a final decision about trusting Jesus. They would go and check on Haji while the young girl was away at work, then invite the grandfather for tea and a private talk. They knew he wanted to say yes to Jesus, but they also knew he cared for his granddaughter more than anything else. He was stalling for her sake.

Finally, they realized that Haji had something he wanted to say to Alifaz. "Men, we have both already made our decision to bring Jesus in our lives. We also know you are leaving. Alifaz, I want you to promise that you will come back for Sonja."

Alifaz gasped for a second and could not speak. Asgat knew how Alifaz felt about Sonja and gave him an elbow and a nod. So Alifaz agreed. When she returned from her house cleaning chores they met her and she and grandfather Haji prayed for the Lord Jesus to come into their lives.

Asgat and Alifaz had completed their assignment of introducing every soul in the village to Jesus. Now they would become MLSTs. Everything was done except a few goodbye tears from Sonja.

Arjand and Ravi received the news about their completion of their project and arrived at the village and contacted the two Lifestory tellers. They found the villagers all willing to give testimony of the Lord as their savior. Some could tell the Lifestory well, and a few had told the Lifestory to others outside the village.

The rain was keeping them mostly confined to the village. It had been raining far too long, and people were starting to worry. Arjand was particularly concerned because the Tawi river was likely to flood. The river was far below this mountain village, but his brother was down there somewhere and had failed to report in.

At last Arjand and Ravi sent Asgat and Alifaz off with commendations of a job well done. They would take the road upward toward the mountain passes and on toward Kishtwar. They would be tested by life as MLSTs.

It was dark before Ravi and Arjand could finish congratulating the villagers and wishing them all the best in their new lives with Jesus. They returned to the house where the Tellers had stayed on the west side of the village near the trail toward Aknoor.

Arjand was restless. He sensed something was wrong with his brother. The men went to bed, but were unable to sleep. Something felt odd. Finally, the feeling was so strong they got up, left the house, and began to walk down the trail. The night was dark because of the rain, and they could not see well. They felt a strange vibration on the ground as they walked along the trail, but did not know why.

They traveled through the night. Upon reaching the town, they drew close to a *dhaba that was open*[11]and asked for tea. It was there they heard the news. The rain had loosened the slope where the village was, and it had completely given way. The entire village had slipped over the ridge and into the canyon below. It was reported that no one had survived. Both men were deeply affected. Arjand became even more troubled about his brother, who was missing in another part of the country.

As the day dawned, more reports began to arrive. All the large rivers of Kashmir were experiencing major flooding. Still more rain was predicted, and this would likely produce the worst flooding in known history. Pictures were coming out of Jammu. The tallest tower near the Tawi was the Hindu temple on the southeast side of the river in Jammu. Only the very tip of the tower could be seen.

The river was raging, tearing at itself in a foaming madness. Sometimes an animal could be seen in the dark brown water being mercilessly thrashed in the roaring waves. Men were standing much too close, as if hypnotized by the sight and sound. Some were looking for their loved ones, to no avail. Thousands had died.

---

[11] Dhaba. A roadside restaurant or truck stop.

The situation was just the same along the Jhelum River in Srinagar. The rain kept coming, along with reports of loved ones last seen being pulled away from life by the churning water.

Coach's mother had a home in the valley and the water was over her house. After the flood subsided, they found her body behind the house, in the mud where the garden had been. Arjand's brother, mother, and father were also lost in the flood.

Alifaz and Asgat, the two new MLST's were on their way to Kishtwar, so it would be some time before they would hear of the loss of the village, along with Sonja and her grandfather. Many Lifestory tellers and their relatives were lost in the flood. We trust they are in the hands of the Lord.

At last the rain stopped. People in the area embraced each other and cried. They were grateful to have a living person to hang on to, assuring themselves that life would continue. It took months to get things back in order. Lifestory teams were busy helping people all over the state of Kashmir to recover from the flood.

Asgat and Alifaz who were the two new MLSTs, had narrowly escaped when they left the village on the hillside where Sonja and her grandfather perished. When they finally learned of the tragedy, they were grateful to the Lord for allowing them the privilege of bringing eternal life to everyone there before the whole village perished. Alifaz mourned for the loss of his dear Sonja and dreamed of seeing her in heaven.

KISHTWAR LAND OF PROMISE

Kishtwar has a reputation of being haunted and full of demons. Legend tells of a traveler who took shelter for the night in a well-known cave there. After falling asleep, he had wild dreams of a strange looking woman who ordered him around and demanded he eat a very sour soup. When he awoke, he had long hair and whiskers, and his clothes were tattered. He had been asleep for a year!

Asgat and Alifaz were undisturbed by Kishtwar's reputation. What they experienced during the floods had cemented their confidence in God's care and His plan for their future.

Asgat reached down, picked up a small, round stone, and tossed it into the stream. He heard the *kaploosh* of the stone hitting the water, then said to Alifaz, "We don't have to know what will happen to us nor how effective we will be. We have Jesus, His Word, and the Lifestory. God has a plan for us, and it is good."

The hike to Kishtwar became more arduous. At first there was only a scattering of small trees and bushes; then they began seeing larger trees. After an hour or so, they came into the forest. The tall trees gave more shade, and it was cooler.

The stream had dwindled to less than half the size it had been when they started. It could easily be crossed with a jump, but there was no need, as they soon came upon a small, well-made bridge of flat stones. They were clearly going the right way.

The forest opened up. Now they could see some distance ahead as the hills had retreated on either side, and a valley lay before them. The grass was shorter due to some grazing cattle. The hikers smelled smoke and heard the tinkling sound of a cowbell.

Surely there were people around here somewhere.

Without warning, three men appeared directly in front of them.

"Stop right now!" one shouted. "Who are you, and what do you want?"

Asgat replied humbly but clearly, "We are teachers, sir."

The man shouted again, "We don't want any teachers. Go away, or we will kill you!"

The young men looked at each other and wondered what they should do.

"Wait," Asgat said. "If you have children, we have a story to tell them."

"What kind of story do you have?"

"It is a beautiful story about God."

For a moment all was quiet; then the elders slowly came closer. They stared at the young men.

The tallest, and possibly the oldest, addressed them, "You may come to our school and tell the children your story, but then you must leave immediately."

Asgat and Alifaz smiled. Asgat put out his hand to the taller man, who reached out and shook it.

Asgat gave a customary greeting, and the man reciprocated. He turned and said, "Follow us, but stay behind us all the time."

They walked together for another half hour. The path became well worn, with many footprints of both people and work animals. The scattered houses they passed were made of logs and clay plaster. The school was in a clearing, surrounded by a rail fence. There was no gate, but a strong pole lay to the side of the fence, ready to close the opening if needed.

After a short discussion at the edge of town, the elders agreed that the young men could come and speak to the school children. They waited outside the school while the two Lifestory tellers addressed the children and their teacher. Over fifteen minutes passed before they emerged from the building, surrounded by children!

The Lifestory tellers had told the Lifestory right away. Both the teacher and her students had responded with a very enthusiastic yes. Asgat and Alifaz led them all in the commitment prayer, then congratulated them on becoming born again. The teacher was so impressed with these two Lifestory tellers that she decided to dismiss her class for the rest of the day. Now the Lifestory tellers were like shepherds with a flock of sheep that followed them wherever they went.

An elder in the town invited Asgat and Alifaz to his house for a cup of tea. They entered the house and sat for tea and roti. Past the kitchen stove was a doorway to another room, with its own window to the outside. As they finished, Asgat asked what was in the other room.

"That is where my daughter stays. She is bedridden and has not walked for over ten years." Sarah was fourteen years old and had not walked since she was four and the day her mother died.

Asgat immediately asked permission to pray for her and tell her the Lifestory. The man said he would be pleased if they would do this.

Asgat told the Lifestory. As he finished, they all heard a strange, loud thump, and the window curtain parted as if something had left in a rush of air. Asgat and Alifaz later reported that they knew something had happened, but they didn't know what.

Upon hearing the Lifestory, the father and the daughter said yes to trusting Jesus to save them. Both committed to follow Jesus.

The time came for the two young men to leave. As customary in the area, the father thanked them for coming, then invited them to stay and have more to eat. They accepted.

When they finished, Asgat and Alifaz left the home and found that many from the town had gathered nearby.

Then the crowd saw Sarah was standing at the door!

Some gasped to see her walking. She approached Asgat and Alifaz and asked them if she could go with them. They declined, but they encouraged her to follow Jesus and to write or call if she had the time.

She would not forget this day it was the day she was healed and the day she met the Lord Jesus.

The young men did a great work in the Kishtwar area and reported regularly to Ravi and Arjand.

SARAH LEARNS TO RUN

Within a year, Sarah contacted Asgat again and asked if there was a way she could learn the Lifestory and begin to tell it to others. Asgat assured Sarah that this was possible.

Without delay, Asgat contacted Ravi, Arjand, and Coach, who contacted the women's team in Jammu. The leader of the women's team was Haji Saab's wife. She told Coach the team was already holding training sessions, so it would be no problem to train Sarah.

Sarah came to Jammu to become a Lifestory teller. The women's team surrounded her with loving support, and Mdm. Zami volunteered to watch over her and keep her while she took the training.

When she finished the training, Sarah returned home, where she decided to teach several other young women the Lifestory. These ladies were motivated by Sarah's adventurous spirit. They quickly learned the Lifestory from her. Now a team of seven, they hoped to serve the Lord by going out to homes in the secluded areas of the mountains to the north and west.

Her village asked lots of questions about this idea. Sarah and the team prayed, asking Jesus for direction. How were they going to do this? His answer was simple: they were to go to each of the remote houses, tell the people what they were doing, and explain that they were doing it for the Lord.

They were to ask for just one thing from every home they would enter. They were convinced that the Lord was telling them to ask the head of each household for an egg, and only for an egg. With this answer from the Lord, Sarah gathered the women, and they left for their field of service.

In a little while, they came to the first house and were invited in. Sarah told the residents about their plan, then told them the Lifestory. It was thrilling to see the family there come to the Lord.

Sarah obeyed the Lord and asked the leader of the home for an egg. They were given an egg and much more. In fact, they never got just an egg from any home they visited. The women received their full support of everything they needed. As they went, they made the Lord famous throughout the region.

More than a year went by, and Sarah was doing well, but she was not finished. She wanted to see Asgat again. It was meant to be. In less than a year, they met again. Sarah captured Asgat's heart, and many began to pray for them to be married.

The wedding was in Kishtwar. More than seven thousand people came to celebrate with them! The Lifestory tellers brought gifts and food and stayed for days.

As a wedding present, the Lifestory tellers decided to dedicate their skill in telling the Lifestory to introduce as many to Jesus as they could in a four-day period.

Asgat had mentioned a particular area that had yet to be visited, so they went there. They spent four days telling the Lifestory. If any demons were left in the area, they were surely put on notice. The Lifestory tellers reported back with many stories of people excited to meet the Lord Jesus.

The newlyweds settled in Kishtwar and prayed for wisdom. But how would they serve Jesus as Lifestory tellers? They decided to start a small English-language school near their village.

Sarah became pregnant, and their daughter was born at the Jammu hospital. Her name is Aaisa. Lifestory tellers from all over heard about the birth and sent gifts. In fact, most of them sent the same gift. Aaisa received ninety-two pink baby gowns! We are still laughing together about this.

We always pray for Asgat and Sarah. They are pioneers in a new area, and they are having their second child soon. Asgat was asked if their next child was to be a boy or a girl. He replied that it has to be a girl because they still have a lot of those baby gowns left over.

As outsiders, we can enter their world only for a moment. In this glimpse, with the Spirit of Jesus Christ, we can feel their joy of commitment and service to the Lord.

THE HEALING HAND OF JESUS

Not only was the Lifestory spreading at an amazing pace but it was also revealing God's power to heal desperately broken lives as well.

DOCTORS TO THE RESCUE

Dr. Jabi began her new life as a Lifestory teller in Jammu by telling the Lifestory to patients who were suffering from depression and mental anxiety. She observed a dramatic change in the patients when they heard and responded to the Lifestory.

Her success was noticed by some of her colleagues. The mental ward in her city was struggling with an increase in women who had been battered and mistreated. They were glad to hear that she was having some success in bringing them out of their depression.

One morning Dr. Jabi heard a moaning sound coming from the garden in front of her house. It reminded her of a dove's cooing. Rushing to her front porch, she was shocked by what she found.

There, in ragged disarray, were the living remains of six battered women. The doctors at the mental ward had attached a note, explaining that their cases were hopeless. No medicines or therapies could heal the damage that had been inflicted upon them. Sometimes the most delicate and beautiful teacups are the most easily broken. Like broken treasures, these women were utterly crushed.

Overcome with compassion, Dr. Jabi took the six ladies in and refreshed them the best she could. She learned they had been raped, tortured, and abandoned. They had become outcastes, losing their family and friends. It was more than they could handle, and they cried constantly.

It would have been easy to despair but knowing the only One who could still help these women, Dr. Jabi told the Lifestory to each of them. She told it again and again.

Slowly, Dr. Jabi watched Jesus go to work in these broken lives. The women began to improve. Several weeks went by while the doctor provided gentle acceptance as she prayed for her patients. Her methods may not have been traditional, but the results spoke for themselves. Dr. Jabi had pioneered a new treatment for mental health.

To give their minds something good to focus on, Dr. Jabi began to teach them the Lifestory. Before long, Dr. Jabi sensed a new strength among them. Her discipline was constant—always loving and positive. Her partnership with Jesus Christ was bringing the crushed ladies back to life.

The ladies began to understand that their participation was of great importance. Learning the Lifestory was one thing, but telling it to another person was much harder. There could be no pushing; each would have to try it in their own time. Perhaps they could tell someone who was in a coma or who was asleep or maybe tell it to a pet. With effort and practice, they began to succeed.

The ladies continued to heal. They got better and better until one day they went together to tell the Lifestory ta a person at a tea stall. It was their first venture out into the outside world. The positive response helped them prove to themselves that they were recovering. It was therapeutic. It was the power of truth over the power of darkness. Together they led another person to Jesus!

For those willing to consider alternate treatment methods, this was an important discovery. News of Dr. Jabi's results quickly reached the ears of those in her city who were also trying to work with such badly abused women.

Dr. Farci

Dr. Farci worked in one of the nearby hospitals. She heard the Lifestory and received the Lord, believing on the Lord's promise to come to her, save her, and never leave her. When she looked up to the Lord like the people looked up to the serpent on the pole, she saw the truth about Jesus being punished in her place. She learned of His power to overcome death itself, and now she believes that He will ever keep her safe. She has a passion to follow the Lord. She called to God through Jesus, and God entered her life.

Dr. Farci heard about the results Dr. Jabi was having with the mental patients. "This is interesting," she told Dr. Jabi. "Would you be interested in bringing this treatment to our hospital?"

After some discussion, Dr. Jabi agreed. She would take ten patients who were suffering from severe depression and try the treatment for one week. After this she would then check the results.

At the end of the week all ten ladies showed signs of improvement. In just three weeks they were doing so well they were released from inpatient care to their normal daily activities with some follow up.

The doctors received unanimous positive feedback from the patients and family and friends. The ladies were well and healthy; best of all they were enduring and becoming Lifestory tellers. This was truly a win win situation.

When Dr. Jabi and Dr. Farci were caring for distressed people they agreed saying: "We aim to tell the Lifestory as early as possible. Frequently we are able to see an immediate improvement in their attitude toward life and in how they face everyday challenges." These reactions are recognizable and in line with both of the doctors' findings.

Mdm, Zami leads

MDM. ZAMI

Mdm. Zami is a prime example of Christ indwelling His servant. She was one of the first women to embrace a commitment to secure one hundred yeses to the Lifestory. Her resolve was illustrated by the very large book she carried.

Mdm. Zami is not a large person, actually she was little and short, but her love for Jesus was very big. It was startling to see her with a big book, nearly three feet long, two and a half feet wide, and two inches thick. The first few pages were full of the names of individuals that said yes to the lifestory when she told it to them. She counts it as a trophy for Jesus. Every entry is complete with a picture and the date and time that they crossed from death to life. When I met her, she had well over three hundred souls listed within those pages.

The next time I heard of Mdm. Zami's book, it was full, front to back, with thousands of names. She had picked a big book because she had a big goal.

What makes Mdm. Zami so special? First, she has an angel at home. Her daughter Angel is also a wonderful Lifestory teller.[12] Mdm. Zami's son is a young man now. He had been in her care because he has been physically challenged since birth. Jerri and I know him and are grateful for his life. Both children are special gifts, like their mother. Mdm. Zami cares for everyone who comes into her life. No one is left behind.

In one situation, Mdm. Zami was sent to help the widows' team in the valley. Her assignment was to bring the poverty-stricken ladies some hope from Jesus in the form of gifts and money from the teams.

---

[12] Angel's story continues in chapter 86.

Hope is scarce in some parts of the country, but Mdm. Zami finds and gives it freely, so much so that the dear ladies called her Mother.

The following testimony is from Mdm. Zami's own words, included here so you can appreciate her dedication to Christ and her words of encouragement to Dr. Farci:

Dear Dr. Farci,

Love to you. We remember your honest labor for *Isa*[13] with the Lifestory as you endured the worst situations in Kashmir. All Lifestory tellers are captives of His eternal love, so I want to share with you my feelings. A few years back, I heard the Lifestory. I was living a meaningless life.

To be honest, I was sinking in a pool of sins and no prophet, *bhagwan*,[14] saint, or anyone was there to extend his hand to get me out of the pool. In the most amazing five minutes of my life, I heard the Lifestory from Brother Awan. It changed my life. Tears poured from my eyes when I said yes to Isa. My whole being was shaking, and I knew I was at the start of a spiritual journey. The Lifestory was a beginning for me, as if time had stopped and started again.

In my sin, Isa had to die for me and give His perfect life for me. He loved me so much that He paid for my life of mistakes with his precious blood. Adam and Eve, through disobedience, lost His fellowship and died spiritually, and they started dying physically. I died instantly with sin and started living in the Holy Spirit when I came to Jesus.

Moses lifted the serpent to save Israelites, and my journey continues through the Lifestory as I lift up Jesus and bring lost sheep to beloved Isa, and He gathers them with great joy.

My journey continues, and I am experiencing many different people. Some with pride, money, knowledge, position, and programs. They all must be born again to know God's kingdom. I tell the

---

[13] *Isa* is the Arabic way of saying Jesus.

[14] A *bhagwan* (also spelled *bhagavan*, *bhagvān*, or *bhagawan*) is a fully enlightened spiritual leader.

Lifestory, and with every yes answer to the Lifestory He multiplies my joy.

In my spiritual journey, every time I tell the Lifestory and get a yes to Isa I am filled with faith, hope, and love. I have faith in Isa, and as I witness Him, I always win souls for him. I hope that many receive Him through the Lifestory and that they will be in heaven with me.

The Lifestory tellers tell everyone about His everlasting love. We all were sinners. And in order to give us eternal life, he gave us His!

So, dear Dr. Farci, we Lifestory tellers have no other mission but to tell the Lifestory and to fulfill His Great Commission by bringing souls to Isa.

We all appreciate and honor your great labor with the Lifestory because you share it with the needy, injured, tortured, abused, mentally hurt, hopeless, and helpless brothers and sisters.

We all pray for you and your fellow Lifestory tellers that every day you may experience more of Isa.

Focusing on Teams

God raised up an additional leader as He prepared to spread Lifestory movements in more territories.

Manjit the Sikh in action

Manjit bound for glory

Manjit the Sikh

This story starts in another dhaba. Coach and a learner had stopped for tea along the road to Amritsar. A nice young man with a Sikh turban served them. His name was Manjit. Coach had a couple of friends with him, so he introduced them to Manjit. He then told the Lifestory to Manjit, who came readily to Jesus and promised to follow Him.

Sikhs are good at keeping their promises, and Manjit was no exception. He began to follow Jesus with great passion, like the frantic hustle of someone who woke up late for work.

Manjit was part owner of the dhaba, which meant he had a big responsibility but a small wage. Three days later he decided to leave the dhaba for good, as he now had a more significant job.

His best friends, whom he had lived with as family for the previous seventeen years, were now back in Amritsar. Now it was urgent that he see them, as he had a very important story to tell them. The telling went well, and his adoptive brothers became born again and are now now his spiritual brothers.

While in Amritsar, it was essential that he visit one other person. Manjit had been assigned a marriage partner since he was a child. In that culture, he was permitted to visit her in her family's home. He went straight to the house, where he found Artie waiting for him. She could see that he had something important to tell her. Excitedly, he told her the Lifestory. She did more than accept Jesus for she fell in love with Him. Her husband to be had done the right thing.

TEAMS ACCELERATE HARVEST

Manjit was progressing so well as a Lifestory teller that Coach told me about him. It is common in the Kashmir area for new tellers to bring in many souls because their goals are high. And Manjit was particularly hasty and devoted. But the Lifestory leaders reported that Manjit was hurrying so fast to share with new people personally that he was not starting teams.

The Lord's wisdom, demonstrated in the Lifestory movements, is that multiplication accelerates when teams form and work together. Teams and their members sharpen each other by affirming the story Jesus is writing through each member of the team. Like a collection of mirrors, each reflects Jesus as He is transforming their lives and teaching them to be fishers of men. Team members see Jesus in each other, and the encouragement and community they enjoy stirs them to multiply.

The question Coach and I then considered was this: How can we encourage Manjit to form and multiply teams without dampening his spirit and possibly slowing him from winning others?

In our inexperience leading such a movement, the thought came that a small nudge toward multiplying teams offered by a person of influence might work. So Coach lined up an appointment for me to meet with Manjit at a Pizza Hut. I was eager to meet him.

I recognized Manjit immediately, even though I had been given no physical description. He was a muscular young man with a black turban and a mustache. As he pushed through the glass doors, I rose from the bench I was sitting on.

As his dark eyes caught mine, he started to kneel. I immediately reached out and caught his hand, urging him upright.

"No, don't kneel! I am the same as you. We are equal in the Lord!"

Manjit rose to his feet, and Coach formally introduced us.

We conversed for a while and ate a pizza. Manjit asked me if there was anything I would like him to do. He assured me he would do it.

I wondered, *Is this a good time for a little nudge?*

I knew Manjit had reported witnessing to thirty two who were solidly following Jesus, so I asked, "How many teams do you have?"

"Twelve," he replied, but he was not understanding what we meant by a team.

I asked naively, "Would you try doubling that number?"

He said: "Yes."

A month later I asked Coach how Manjit was doing and how many teams he had. The news was that He was working hard to win more souls and that his count was about doubled.

When Coach asked him, He said: "Thirty!" I was puzzled at this and asked was that the amount of people, or teams? He had won an additional thirty people and that gave him enough by counting two people to be a team to have thirty teams. That was a mistake of me getting into something I had no reason to be in. That should all have been done by the local leaders.

The Lifestory leadership had defined a team simply as two or more persons. Had Manjit simply divided the number of his new Lifestory tellers to create new teams so he could report double their number to me? I would later find that he was doing all he could to do the right thing. His trial was to learn how to develop a team.

I asked Coach if this was the case. He said: "Yes, Manjit may be trying to help new Lifestory tellers gather in productive teams, but his approach doesn't seem natural."

I asked the Lord to forgive me for trying to nudge Manjit. I had confused him into increasing his reported number of teams by simply dividing the number of people who had said yes to following Jesus.

Manjit did not need nudging; he needed vision and modeling. Wonderfully, God was already working to arrange these and Manjit already had enough on his mind with his upcoming wedding. It was not right to burden him with forming teams when he himself had not yet been a part of one.

My lesson was about my position. Here I was serving them and thinking I knew a better way. The reality is my serving needs to be enlightened through Jesus. My craftiness or education was not what he needed. He needed the ground support of people he rubbed shoulders with every day. He needed people who understand his culture, language and family heritage, and the people he knows as friends because these are the ones who can watch his back and see a way to overcome because they had to overcome. And they are best prepared to cover him and protect him.

My immediate service must be focused on the people God has called into range near me on a regular basis and who have the same burden for souls. This is not saying he was not burdened for souls. This is about the transmission of vision. Very little happens until this is accomplished and perceived to be a mutual calling between partners, or fellow laborers willing to commit. I had to grow up to serve. It takes time and devotion to the Lord and to the ones we commit to serve. I must also be alert and watching for better ways to serve the glory of God. It is easy to see the mistakes of others and complain, but real forward motion comes when it costs us more than we planned on giving, then for Jesus we step forward. Like Manjit.

LEARNING TO FORM TEAMS

Not long after Manjit and Artie married, they traveled to Jammu. We believe it was from the Lord that they were there in time to hear the testimony of Raj Kumar. His wife was the one Coach saved from drowning in an earlier chapter. Raj had become a leader, establishing teams in Jaipur and Himachal Pradesh. His ability to develop teams was evident, and Manjit took notice. Now Manjit would learn from Raj Kumar by working with him in the Himachal Pradesh area.

The harsh climate meant there were few comforts along the way, but Manjit and his bride went to work introducing souls to Jesus from village to village, from one end of the valley to the other. Eventually, the pathways became so covered with snow that the team had to walk on the ice along the edge of the river. It was here their resolve was challenged past their limits.

Dear Artie's feet froze. As soon as transportation was available, she was taken to the hospital. Many prayed for her healing, including teams from Kashmir to East India and even in the United States. Love floods the hearts of the Lifestory tellers when they see and hear of the sacrifice of these dear champions.

Every day more and more people asked God to protect and heal Artie's feet. When word came that she was beginning to recover and would eventually be all right, everyone felt great relief. God kept watch over these two wonderful people. Wherever they went, difficulties and trials turned into great and mighty works of God.

SAMARITAN ANGELS

About a year later, Manjit and Artie decided to organize and support a general conference of Lifestory tellers in the Haryana area. They were bringing supplies for the conference on their motorcycle, including hundreds of copies of the Lifestory for the teachers' training. The road was dark, and sharp curves lay ahead. Just a few yards of road soon changed their lives.

A car approaching from the opposite direction was going far too fast for the curve. Unable to keep to his lane, the driver slammed into Manjit and Artie, sending them and their bike crashing off the road into the darkness. The bike was mangled, and they were badly injured.

The driver sped away without stopping to check on them. Chances were slim that anyone would soon come along, let alone see them where they lay in the brush off the side of the road. They needed an angel from heaven, and they needed it immediately.

God sent several angels riding motorcycles. These bikers were truly Good Samaritans. They made it their habit to travel this lonely road and watch for those who had the misfortune of being stranded along the way.

Manjit was soon tied behind one of the riders and rushed to the hospital while several others stayed with Artie. At the hospital, Manjit was rushed to the emergency room. A car was sent back to pick up Artie, and she was brought to the hospital as well. Manjit and Artie had been saved!

The Lord helped Manjit and Artie when they were suffering, and He turned this tragedy into a dream come true for these wonderful Bikers. Some of the bikers stayed with them at the hospital. Others hired a truck to retrieve the crumpled bike and conference materials.

The bikers gathered nearly all the training materials and brought some of the copies to Manjit. When he realized what they had done, he was very thankful. Some of the men who had helped him then said, "Tell us about these papers."

Manjit couldn't have imagined a better opening! These bikers were about to be born again.

Good came from misfortune over and over for Manjit and Artie. Just like Joseph in the Bible, the Lord turned all the evil they encountered into good.

Manjit and Artie continued serving, and God's glory increased moment by moment as Jesus was lifted along the byways. Manjit became a team builder. He taught the bikers the Lifestory. They grew in Christ and became a strong team called the highway team. As the team grew in number, the highways along the Grand Trunk Road became their field of service, including part of Rajasthan and the Punjab. It is now common to find dhabas along these routes, offering a free cup of tea and the Lifestory.

MIRACLE BIRTH

While Manjit and Artie were focused on doing something special with Jesus, we were wondering what great thing God would do next with them. We believed with them that it is a great thing to have children. The Bible describes children as gifts from God, like arrows in a man's quiver and olive plants around his table. Now it was time for Artie and Manjit to have their first child.

The hospital was crowded, and the ward for expectant mothers had few available beds. Artie was placed in a bed beside a Muslim lady whom the doctors had been watching carefully. Artie had little time to visit before an attendant stopped to see the lady beside her.

The attendant showed the lady a report and told her that her baby wasn't moving. They were concerned the child might be dead. Even if it was still alive, the delivery was going to be very dangerous for her. The inactivity was becoming more alarming, and the options were worsening as time went on.

Understandably, the lady was distraught. Artie prayed for her and tried to calm her. She even asked the lady to listen to a short story, and she agreed. Upon hearing the Lifestory, the lady said yes to Jesus and prayed desperately for the Lord to come into her life. Within a short time, the lady reported that her baby was moving!

The situation rapidly improved after she believed in the Lord for her salvation. She had the baby with a natural birth, and both mother and child came through with no problems.

Artie also had a normal delivery. The arrival of their son, Gurjeet, became the newest and most exciting event in Manjit's and Artie's lives.

Terror in the Telling

This next event may seem a little disheartening, so please remember that everything works for good for those who love God and are called according to His purpose.

Manjit and Artie, their baby, and two new Lifestory tellers, Tariq and Rakis, had traveled along the highway to an area in the mountains. It was a hot day in the lower country, so they enjoyed being where it was cool. At one point where the highway was level, a pullout offered a place for people to stop and take a break.

Manjit was teaching the two men how to approach people and tell the Lifestory, and this was a good place for them to practice. They had engaged with several people who were interested in hearing it.

The road was wide, and there was an adjacent parking area. It was a common place for impatient drivers to endanger bystanders by trying to pass slower vehicles. Pedestrians had to be extra attentive there.

Overtaking a vehicle in India is difficult. Frequently, a slow driver in front will speed up when they realize someone is trying to get by them. This may have caused what happened next.

A truck was approaching the level area and was hoping to move a few spaces forward by passing a vehicle or two. Moreover, the truck was both overweight and top-heavy. The driver had gathered his speed and pulled out to pass, when he realized that an approaching vehicle was on a crash course with his truck.

The truck was barely past one vehicle when the driver swerved to escape a head-on collision. A sudden swerve is not a good thing for a speeding, top-heavy truck! The driver now had to swerve back to stay in his lane. The truck continued swerving back and forth until the driver lost control altogether, and the truck careened off the road.

On the side of the road, the team was telling the Lifestory. Their attention was on the people they were addressing. Artie stood slightly behind them, holding the baby. Suddenly, Rakis dashed past her, away from the road. Artie turned and hastily jumped out of the way of the truck that was now traveling on two wheels.

In less than a second, the truck seemed to fall from the sky on Manjit and Tariq. The terrible noise of the crash turned to silence; then the horror sunk in. In shock and fear, Artie and Rakis struggled to breathe.

Some of the truck's load was spread around the parking area, but there was no sign of Manjit or Tariq. They could only be lying beneath the truck and the remaining cargo. The bystanders jumped into action, unloading the truck as fast as possible. Minutes seemed like hours. Finally, the men gathered around the topside of the truck and began to lift it slowly back to an upright position.

There on the pavement lay the two men, like broken vases wrapped in cloth and a turban. An ambulance rushed them to the hospital nearly forty minutes away. Both were alive, but they were comatose. Manjit had severe head injuries. Tariq also had head trauma, but the damage to his throat and chest was worse. We waited and prayed for any word on their condition.

It was several weeks before Tariq came out of his coma. For more than a month, he could not speak. He could only make little sounds. It took many months of therapy before he regained normal speech.

Over a month later, Manjit was still unconscious. The doctors said he would have a terrible scar on his face and then he added, if he survives.

We continued to lift both men to the Lord in prayer. The Lord heard our prayers, and Manjit was returned to us. He had trouble speaking, but he improved with therapy and time. He was told he might always have slurred speech because of the injuries to his mouth.

But Manjit is an overcomer, and with the help of the Lord he regained most of his abilities. The scar on his face was soon covered by a nice, healthy beard. Thanks to God, Manjit and Tariq were back with us again. These men would not give up because the Lord had given them a sense of destiny. Stopping their mission was inconceivable.

MANJIT FIRST PLACE FISHER OF MEN

A few years later, some of the team leaders were prompted by the Lord to accelerate their activity with the Lifestory. They came together in October for a leaders' conference. At this meeting, they recalled that they had missed many opportunities over the years to tell the Lifestory to people they knew.

Many friends and relatives had died without being invited to follow Jesus. One Lifestory teller stood and named four close friends and a neighbor who had died without trusting Jesus because he had neglected to share the good news. This concern grew into a call for action through a complete attitude change among the Lifestory tellers.

The leaders circulated a notice to all the Lifestory teams of Kashmir, urging them to change the way they thought about leading the lost to Jesus, from "necessary" to "urgent." To stir those who agreed, the Kashmir Lifestory teams held a competition to see which teams would bring the most souls to Jesus Christ by the end of November. The increase in souls won would be a present for Christ's birthday.

We received a video showing Manjit in front of the hospital in Kashmir, where he worked with his small Lifestory team for the month of November. Manjit's team brought 524 people to trust Jesus. Some of these became Lifestory tellers and were trained to teach others to tell the Lifestory. Manjit's vision is great, and the Lifestory tellers love him.

The teams in Kashmir have agreed to continue considering it urgent to reach everyone with the Lifestory.

LEADING SIKHS TO JESUS

In North India, the Lifestory movement is shaped by the Lord through His Word and through one another. Manjit wanted to introduce many from his Sikh community to the Lord. He suggested a monthlong plan to share Jesus with them, with the help of teams from the area.

The month's theme was Matthew 6:33: "Seek first his kingdom and his righteousness, and all these things will be given to you as well." All were ready to take on the effort. They felt it was the kind of thing Jesus would do, and it was the kind of thing they could put their heart into as people who seek the Kingdom of God first.

Manjit is a good example of someone seeking first the Kingdom of God in northern Kashmir. In this seeking, he has been called to be a catalyst. The teams have given him the name "Light post for Jesus."

Three hours before sunrise, four days a week, Manjit cleans three Sikh temples (*dracas*). He no longer worships there; he follows Jesus now. Yet every day he cleans the toilets and the many floors and tables. He also prepares the tea and biscuits that will be served later. He works very hard to complete his task before lunchtime; then he goes about the city fulfilling his calling as a master Lifestory teller.

The plan to share Jesus with the Sikh community was taking shape. Members of Manjit's team and friends and members of several other teams all worked together, including the women's team. Mdm. Zami played a significant part, especially when it came to organizing and training the women who came to the Lord.

The event took place in the Pathankot District, about sixty miles southeast of Jammu. Everyone was telling the Lifestory in their respective area. They had asked the Lord to give the district a hub of dedicated and active servants for the Lord to continually tell the Lifestory. Their daily trips brought them closer to this goal.

The first part of the plan was completed in less than a week. Manjit and the teams had introduced even more people to Jesus than they had hoped. They then formed a new team of local Lifestory tellers dedicated to following Jesus. These new Lifestory tellers were encouraged to select a leader who would oversee the team and report back to Manjit and Mdm. Zami. They especially hoped to produce a teacher who could teach the Lifestory to new Lifestory tellers in the area.

The goals were reached and then surpassed. An estimated seven hundred people heard the Lifestory and trusted the Lord for salvation. Of those individuals, approximately three hundred took the Lifestory-teller training. Most of them could tell the Lifestory and were eager to do so. The MLSTs served the new Lifestory tellers, giving them tips and encouragement to help them reach their goal of active service to the Lord. Approximately forty of those trained were striving to get one hundred yeses so they could qualify to apply for master-level training.

Perhaps the best way to decrease the time needed for a candidate to reach one hundred yeses is to guide them in recruiting and training those they lead to Jesus to also become Lifestory tellers. The yeses achieved this way by our disciples also counted toward our own one hundred yeses. This is a powerful driver of multiplication of the Lifestory movements.

Recruiting and training others takes more initial effort and record keeping. But it teaches responsibility as an essential part of following Jesus and becoming a team leader. It also unifies a team, teaching them to work together for the sake of the Gospel. In the end, three of the Lifestory tellers qualified and were trained as new master teachers.

This new team was now positioned for ongoing multiplication. The new teachers and leaders reported to Manjit and Mdm. Zami. A special prayer group was developed to pray every day for their outreach. In the field, their time of prayer and reading the Word together indicated they would continue to follow the Lord's direction.

The formation of this new team demonstrated God's faithfulness and fulfilled the goal of an ongoing center for dedicated servants who continually serve the Lord with the Lifestory.

EXPANSION

Many of the Lifestory tellers were losing family members to death before they could share the Lifestory with them. Because of this and For Jesus's birthday, they wanted to tell it even more widely and rapidly so they raised the level of how important it was to share the lifestory to urgent. In Jammu they developed a contest from November to Christmas that the team that won the most people to the Lord in that time would be the champion Fishers of Men for that day.

THE FISHING MILKMAID

My grandson Ben is captain of a fishing boat. It was a treat to receive a video of him and his crew of four catching fish. Each one pulled in fish after fish. It was exciting to see how many fish could be harvested by four crew members and a captain. We like to compare our Lifestory teams to these fishers as we become fishers of men and follow our captain, the Lord Jesus Christ.

In India, it is sometimes said that all buildings have at one time been atop of the head of a woman. This is how many heavy loads are carried in India up the stairs and ladders to build most structures. .

Soni had a large bucket of buffalo milk balanced on her head. She tooted a small handheld horn and walked with perfect posture to the front of a customer's house. Two kilos of milk from her bucket was the normal order for this household.

Arjand met her at the door, confirmed his usual order, and thanked her as he handed her payment. Not many come to Arjand's house without hearing the Lifestory. This day he said to her:"Miss, I have a short story. It is about five minutes long. Would you like to hear it?"

The wobble is one signal for yes in India. Soni's wobble was slight because of her bucket, but Arjand knew she was agreeing. For her sake, he told the Lifestory quickly. Her yes was immediate.

In this culture, women only interact with other women regarding spiritual matters, so Arjand gave Mdm. Zami's number to Soni and encouraged Soni to tell Mdm. Zami about her experience with Jesus.

Soni called Mdm. Zami after Soni finished her route that afternoon. To Soni's surprise, Mdm. Zami already knew about her encounter with Jesus. Arjand had told her. It took little convincing for Soni to meet Mdm. Zami over tea.

Soni has a lovely personality, and Mdm. Zami is much the same.

They were so good for each other. By the time Soni and Mdm. Zami finished their first visit, the two ladies were as close as sisters, and Soni was firmly convinced God had a great plan for her life.

The following week, Soni took steps that changed her life forever. First, she received Lifestory training from Mdm. Zami and became an active Lifestory teller. Now she was a bubbling-over milkmaid. Every customer listened to her cheerful way of telling the Lifestory.

Many were saying yes to following Jesus, just like she had. She sent the ladies who said yes to Mdm. Zami for coaching; then she organized the new Lifestory tellers by starting a weekly prayer meeting. Early in the week, she would use her phone to publish the time and place of the meeting.

People were growing in Christ all around her as Mdm. Zami guided her in building a new team. This is now called the Noor team. *Noor* means "the light from heaven."

The Noor team expanded exponentially as Soni learned and applied team building and multiplication principles. She embraced the urging of the Lifestory team leaders to shift her team's perspective on sharing the Lifestory from necessary to urgent, and the Noor team joined the November competition to introduce souls to Christ. As the competition reached its climax, the newly formed Noor team shot from last place to challenge the front runners. With her gifts, talents, and supernatural guidance, Soni was doing very well.

Soni's milk business also began growing exponentially. When she came to the Lord, Soni was selling one can of milk per day, carrying the large bucket on her own head. A good number of the young men with whom she shared the Lifestory also became Lifestory tellers and joined the Noor team. Many of them needed work. All of them came to Jesus.

Soni realized she could expand her business in a way that would help everyone, but young men could not be expected to carry buckets of milk on their heads. Soni had to change the way that milk was delivered.

JON SMITH

URGENCY TAKES OVER

A town full of Lifestory teams with an urgent vision for the salvation of others is like an active beehive. Everyone works together with a keen focus on rescuing the perishing.

In Jammu, the Lifestory teams were systematically distributed throughout the city. One was near the city center, where there were five colleges and a lot of young adults.

Every Lifestory Teller was out sharing hope through the Lifestory in the goodness of God to overcome all evil. As the tellers told the Lifestory to all who would listen. Many came to trust God and find the debt of their sins paid by Jesus Christ.

Sometimes the Lifestory tellers would have tea together, sharing their stories of the great things the Lord was doing.

The people of Jammu were busy, but not too busy to listen for five minutes to a story that would lift up Jesus and usher them into an eternal relationship with Him. Many of them boarded the ship for their journey to the promised land.

What If We Hadn't Obeyed?

Amid our rejoicing, we considered how easily all these victories could have been missed entirely. Jesus told a parable of a few people who were trusted with talents by their Lord. Eventually, their actions were weighed. Several were rewarded for making a profit for their Lord, but one focused on protecting himself and put his talent under a stone. He lost everything.

We could have missed this great harvest entirely if we had focused on ourselves—our inability to speak the language or win arguments or navigate the culture.

As we focused on God rather than ourselves, He had given us the simplest of ways to introduce souls to Jesus: We teach the Lifestory to a few people who speak English. They then tell it to the ones to whom we cannot speak. This works because the Lifestory gives every person who trusts Jesus the ability to immediately be fruitful in sharing Jesus.

It is good to give bread to someone asking for bread, and it is good to do the work of the Lord. But the very first thing we do is bring unsaved people to salvation; then we teach them how to hear and follow Jesus and teach their loved ones to do the same.

For a family to feel safe enough to trust the Lord, believers must approach them with love and respect from their own culture, without arguments and in their own context. We should never be critical of those who are showing signs of trusting Jesus, who may grow in faith to surpass us in faith, hope, and love.

Having witnessed the wonderful acts of the Lifestory tellers in Kashmir, I sometimes wonder, *The Kashmiri are so very hospitable to strangers. How did they miss coming to Jesus for so long?*

LANGUAGE TEST BRINGS
A NEW MINDSET

I was taken by taxi to a mosque on the edge of town. It was my first visit with a moulvi. My language was limited, and I was uncertain how the meeting would go.

The taxi drove onto a single lane dirt road that ran parallel to a canal. We could see the mosque on the other side of the water. A worn trail led down to a small footbridge. The taxi driver parked by the trailhead, and I guessed he was a Muslim familiar with the area.

The moulvi soon came out and crossed the bridge to us. I motioned for him to join me in the back seat of the cab. He got in and sat beside me; then he dismissed the driver to go for a walk.

I knew the Lifestory well, but not in Urdu. It took me more than ten minutes to tell it, as I tried to make sure he understood the main points. He wobbled his head to indicate he understood about Moses, and he said a strong "Hah!" when it came to trusting Jesus.

He followed me in prayer. I congratulated him on becoming born again according to the scriptures. He then hurriedly left, and the driver returned to take me on my way.

As we drove, I prayed and went over the presentation in my mind. I was a bit apprehensive about my limited Urdu. It bothered me. I did feel, however, that he understood the message and that he had accepted Jesus as his own savior. When I got home, I walked into our living room and told Jerri about the experience. She thought it was terrific, so I felt released to celebrate a little.

Two hours later the phone rang. It was Coach. He was excited, but I could only understand that since I left the mosque the moulvi had called him multiple times. What was wrong?

The moulvi had not rejected Jesus. In fact, quite the opposite. He was excited about being born again and was asking Coach question after question about Jesus! Even while we were talking, Coach had to take another call from the moulvi.

The next morning, I met Coach for language class. His report about the moulvi was a real eye-opener. Just since my time with him at the mosque, the moulvi had called Coach more than a dozen times to get more information on Jesus.

"The reason he is asking so much about Jesus," Coach explained, "is because he has four madrasas[15] of schoolchildren he teaches every day. He wants to know what he can tell them about Jesus. He is soaking up everything about the Lord like a sponge."

"Wow!" I said. "The Lifestory is surely a key to sharing the Lord in this Islamic community."

While they have no interest in an outside religion, they do want Jesus. Perhaps they had just not yet heard a nonthreatening presentation of Jesus.

---

[15] A madrasa is a school for Islamic instruction.

SPEEDING TO ETERNAL LIFE

Two young men, ages sixteen and nineteen, were commissioned to share Jesus in remote areas. Nias was nearing his college graduation, and Ajaz needed a new lease on his young life because of his father's tragic passing. They took no bags, and they took no money.

They had quite an adventure! After crossing a river, they ventured far into an unfamiliar land. At times they survived by staying in mosques, where young men could stay for only a few rupees per day. A simple meal was included, along with the possibility of working off payment by helping with cleaning. The arrangement also resulted in good public relations for the mosque.

One bus ride became memorable when Nias confronted the rash driver: "Sir, would you be so kind as to slow down? Your speeding is making all of us fear for our lives."

The driver replied, "I have a schedule, you know. If I don't make it in time, I will have no choice but to loose my employment."

Nias asked: "I have a short story. It is only about five minutes, and it may calm your heart. Would you like to hear it?"

The rash driver replied: "Yes, tell me the story."

By this time, the young man had moved up near the door beside the driver's seat. He held on to the rail and began to tell him the Lifestory. As Nias neared the end of the Lifestory, the driver pulled off to the side of the road and stopped so he could listen without distraction.

After finishing the Lifestory, Nias asked the driver if he wanted to trust Jesus to save him, like the people in front of Moses who believed his instructions were from God and looked up to the serpent on the pole. He responded with a yes. Just as they trusted Moses and looked up and were saved, the driver looked to Jesus to save him. The bus driver then followed Nias in prayer, confirming he trusted the Lord to save him and inviting Jesus to come into his life.

The driver stood and addressed the passengers. "I apologize for driving too fast. This young man has a short story to tell you. It will take a few minutes. Please listen to him."

Nias told the Lifestory again and was amazed to bring in such an unexpected harvest. It was a highlight of their trip, occurring near the end of their journey.

HOSPITALITY, AGED TO PERFECTION

Nias and Ajaz were out of rupees, so they decided to walk home. It would take about a week. By the end of the first day, their route brought them to a small town of scattered dwellings. They followed a path off the road and soon found themselves among the homes of those of meager means.

Abdul Aziz stood in the doorway of his humble hut. He was a dignified man, noble in appearance but clearly acquainted with hard work. He took one look at the two young men coming down the path and recognized them as hungry, tired travelers.

He invited them in, and they accepted. It was easy to see that Abdul and his wife, Zorba, had very little to offer. What they did have they offered freely to the worn and weary youth. Zorba made a soup of everything possible; then she doled out a portion to each. The soup revived the travelers, along with cool water to drink and a pan in which to wash their face and hands. There was no question: they were expected to stay.

Evening came, and they enjoyed the Kashmiri custom of talking well into the night. When Nias told the Lifestory, the stars of heaven twinkled brightly enough to reflect off the tears on Zorba's and Abdul's faces. They understood what Jesus meant when He said he would draw all men to himself. Jesus had taken their death sentence upon Himself and gave them new life.

It wasn't just that they received Jesus that night. They had spent their life together anticipating that He would come to them. They were waiting for this to happen. For them, it was an invitation to a lifetime of prayer. In this spiritually aware time, the four of them relished the presence of the Lord of Peace among them.

Nias and Ajaz found it hard to leave the next morning. With hugs and tears and roti folded in a newspaper, the Lifestory tellers headed home. Their visit with Abdul and Zorba would not be forgotten. Their home was the best hospitality for the boys. It may always remind them of something like a fish broiled on an open fire and served by someone like Jesus.

More Travelers, More Hospitality

Less than a year later, Arjand and his team entered the outskirts of the same small town that Ajaz and Nias had visited. They were thirsty and looking for a source of good water. The hut of the elderly gentleman Abdul stood out as a good place to find. Arjand the Deliverer was known to bring whole communities into the Lord. He came to the same house that Ajaz and Nias had visited.

First he asked, "Is there water nearby?" Then he added, "I have a short story. Would you like to hear it?"

"I also have a short story. Would you like to hear it?"

Arjand gave honor to the elder by asking to hear his story first.

Abdul said, "Today is 2014. Most people understand this."

Both men laughed heartily over wanting to share the same Lifestory.

Abdul and Zorba helped the small team of Lifestory tellers with all that they needed, offering the same hospitality as they had for the two young men who had come earlier. They were glad to hear the latest news about Nias and Ajaz. The young men had not shared the tragic death of Ajaz's father. When Abdul heard this and understood the gravity of Ajaz's situation, his admiration for Ajaz grew even more.

Ajaz's father had gotten into a struggle with some harsh men, and he was killed. A false report was circulated, making it hard for Ajaz and his sisters to stay in their own home. The trip with Nias was intended to help young Ajaz put things back together in his mind. Staying with Abdul and Zorba had been just what Nias and Ajaz needed.

Abdul and Zorba's hospitality for Arjand and his friends was gratefully received. They needed a place to teach new Lifestory tellers, and this was a good place to start.

Things were looking up for Zorba and Abdul. Each Lifestory group who visited them increased their outreach to the town. Other travelers sometimes needed a simple bed and breakfast inn, and they came to value the great company in a family setting.

The older couple supported others in many ways, helping with training new Lifestory tellers and spreading the news about eternal life and the Lord's redemption plan to every person in their small town.

Abdul and Zorba had a remarkable summer. They were so happy that God was with them and that He favored them by bringing an abundance of new friends. Every person who visited them added value to their lives. They likewise added something to those who came.

APPOINTMENT TO KEEP

Abdul cared for Zorba well, but her darkest night was soon to arrive. As they were in their late seventies, they might forget an appointment now and then, but not this one.

Like any other day, they finished their work and went to bed. In the morning, Zorba rose. The sun also rose, but Abdul did not. During the night, he had passed quietly into the arms of Jesus.

Several from the Jammu women's Lifestory team came to help. Mdm. Zami and another woman offered to stay after the funeral.

It was soon evident, however, that Zorba would not falter because of her loss. She wished to be home alone. She returned to the hut that evening, held the blanket, and prayed her prayers. The walls faded into the darkness; there was no reason for a lamp. What she wanted to see could be seen with her eyes closed. The memory of their life of prayer together gave her strength to make a final decision about facing the future without Abdul. From then on, she would become well known as an active Lifestory teller. Zorba would overcome her harsh realities with Jesus.

ZORBA CHALLENGES THE NIGHT

Zorba helps widows and orphans, battered women and rape victims, the destitute and unpopular. She listens and prays. As she organizes women into groups, she watches for ways to help, then encourages them to trust God to meet their needs.

Sometimes Zorba stays with Mdm. Zami, and sometimes she takes relief to needy children in broken homes. Other times she returns to her hut, which she maintains as a place where people can learn to tell the Lifestory or meet together to serve.

Zorba went to Srinagar to shepherd the engagement of a young couple. Many of the Lifestory tellers believed the match was made in heaven, but there were obstacles to the marriage. Mdm. Zami's daughter Angel was familiar with tragedy and had learned to overcome her trials with the help of God and her mother, who has the heart of a lion. Zorba was watching over the young bride-to-be. Their faith would overcome the difficulties.

This was a time for close family members of the groom to examine the potential bride's character and reputation. Each relative could pose questions and give reasons why they were for or against the marriage. This would determine whether the wedding would take place.

The groom was a noted Lifestory teller, accomplished in training and education, in a good trade, and prepared for the responsibilities of marriage. He was deeply in love with the bride, herself a beautiful, young Lifestory teller. But because Angel was fatherless and had little money, some members of the groom's family did not consider Angel a suitable marriage prospect for him.

All the Lifestory tellers who knew Angel were praying for her and the groom. We had already watched the Lord capture her future father-in-law's heart. We were now praying for an uncle who remained opposed to the engagement. He also opposed the Lifestory and the Lifestory tellers. But what happened next was amazing.

Zorba and the women's team leaders prayed for the uncle and asked him to listen to the Lifestory. He laughed and told them that even if he heard the Lifestory nothing would change. Zorba then told him the Lifestory. He said nothing and left for home.

The next morning, this uncle sought Zorba out and told her he had a dream that night in which he saw a great many in white clothes telling the Lifestory, and Zorba was with them. Not only this but his wife and two children had all dreamed the very same dream!

Upon hearing this, Zorba prayed and gave thanks. With the uncle's permission, she told the Lifestory to the entire family. All received Jesus and are now sharing the joy of fellowship and the testimony of their experience with Him.

Haji Saab Enjoys a New Season

Kashmir is very political and very diverse. Each religious and ethnic group has its own way of thinking and living out its beliefs. There are many sides to every issue, and it is common for someone to be offended.

For example, in some places it is a capital offense to transport a buffalo in a vehicle. They would be assigned the same penalty as kidnapping a person. The thinking is that the buffalo would be taken to a part of the state where it could be slaughtered. This would be considered murder by those who eat only vegetables and worship animals.

Such diversity between groups and ideologies requires special qualities of civil servants. They must be able to pursue their own political and ideological agendas while encouraging a common civility.

One of the greatest of these civil servants was Haji Saab, known as a fiery orator with a passion for defending the rights of others. Coach and I were about to approach him with the Lifestory. We had an invitation to talk with him because he and Coach had a close relationship.

A letter of admission into the housing area allowed us through the guard station. Haji Saab's home was just a bit further. As we got out of the car and approached the house, I walked cautiously behind Coach so he would be more visible. I felt it would be best for someone in this secure area to see a familiar face first. Since I would appear as a foreign stranger, I intended to be a quiet foreign stranger. I was praying for this meeting that God would save the souls of Haji Saab and his wife.

Coach rang the gate alarm on the outside wall, and soon a woman appeared. She welcomed us into the courtyard and then into the house. We placed our shoes on the porch near the door before entering.

I had heard from Coach that his uncle was very active and had thought this meant he was younger. Haji Saab was old yet lively. He studied me carefully without appearing rude or alarmed. I posed no threat. We smiled from a distance, and I tried to feel comfortable.

From my point of view, Coach was arranging an appropriate setting for sharing the Lifestory. The way he presented me to his elder highlighted my humanity and my character as a reasonable person. We didn't want Haji Saab to became defensive, so we tried to be harmless but wise.

As the conversation with Haji Saab began, I quickly realized we were still seeking permission to talk with him. As Haji Saab controlled everything, it would be inappropriate to force the subject. Haji Saab wanted to get to know me, but he also wanted the telling of Coach's story to be private—between him and Coach. Coach would have to make another trip to tell the Lifestory to Haji Saab.

I was happy to be there for Coach, and I was glad to meet and visit with Haji Saab. He was a very nice person who I would have liked for a good friend. I respected his careful approach to Coach's requests.

I prayed for Coach because I could see this meant a lot to him. Sometime later we heard that Coach had another appointment with Haji Saab. I knew this would be the business appointment that is our Father's business. We prayed for them, and we prayed for the Lord's will.

As we age, we realize we have fewer options ahead. Haji Saab had no lack of courage. It was his need to trust that kept his heart from responding too quickly. The Lord worked on Haji Saab and brought him to a place where trust could happen. Haji Saab put up no resistance when Coach told him the Lifestory. He welcomed Jesus into his heart. In the end, he came, and we all rejoiced.

Next came the salvation of Haji Saab's devoted wife. After Haji Saab decided to make Christ his savior, Mdm. Zami and the women's team came and brought the Lifestory to her in such a way that she, too, was blessed to see the truth about God's love for her in Jesus. As she listened to His word, Haji Saab's wife understood the strength of Christ's promise to bring her into His salvation. She became very helpful among the female Lifestory tellers.

Victory before Death

The Lifestory offers sinners a clear, non threatening way to respond to the claims of Christ. If we share a complete Gospel with someone, and they say yes and follow Jesus, we rejoice. We believe every person we share with is sent by God. As long as they live, it is possible for them to be saved.

The enemy lost with Haji Saab. His passing came just over a year after he came to Jesus. We were blessed with his efforts to bring more people to salvation because he loved Jesus. He walked with God and won the victory through Christ before he died.

God gave us II Thessalonians 1:7&8 through Apostle Paul. He had lived a life before he met Jesus. He knew very well what it was to be a non believer. How urgent is it for us to love our neighbor as ourselves?

Nargi, Jala, and Sufi Treasure

The music provided by Sufi singers is an integral part of every public event in northern Kashmir. Sometimes, with little apparent reason, they will approach a house and begin to play and sing. They somehow know who is sad or under stress, and they offer comfort.

We believe God sent the two talented Sufi singers to our house that day. Nargi and Jala came to learn how to teach the Lifestory. Coach did the training, and we enjoyed their music after class. The next day they sang the Lifestory song for us. It was exciting to know they planned to sing the Lifestory before every wedding and funeral. Any time they appeared on radio or television, they would start with the song of the Lifestory.

We enjoyed their fellowship and marveled at their enthusiasm. Throughout the years, Nargi and Jala have proven to be emissaries of God's love song to the people of Kashmir. The singers' teams have been spreading God's love far and wide in areas where there are Sufis.

Nargi and Jala organized their Lifestory groups of singers in the same way the international Sufi network is organized in a way that is according to their listeners' needs, their trades, and family traditions.

The livelihood of the singers depends on knowing when community events are happening, so they make friends and listen through the grapevine. For example, when young people are ready for marriage, the singers first plan their participation in the wedding, then approach the couple with their plan. The same happens when a baby is about to be born. One person might be seriously ill, and another might be planning to do Haj. Knowing these needs provides insight and allows the singers to participate on a personal level. They work together for one cause: to bring God's Holy Spirit through music to all the people.

The inclusion of the Lifestory in their repertoire has led to rapid expansion of the singers' teams. The universal need for a second chance at life and the assurance of eternal life through Jesus the Christ guarantees their success. In Christ are all the treasures of wisdom and knowledge. Nargi and Jala were ordained by the Lord to sing the Lifestory.

A STITCH IN TIME

Coach's daughter Mary has grown accustomed to hearing of the great things happening through the Lifestory. She is always looking for opportunities to share it.

One day she went to an area of her town where she noticed a shop called the Stitching Center advertising training for young women.

Mary entered to inquire about the business. A quick look into the back of the building revealed a dozen or so young women working on garments. The proprietor came to the front office to meet her. Mary introduced herself and expressed interest in the shop. The lady told Mary about her great desire to help young women gain a trade and find a way to make a living.

Mary asked her if she would like to hear a short story. When Mary asked if she would have followed Moses's instructions and looked up to the serpent on the pole, she said yes. When she heard that Jesus was calling her to trust Him to save her in the very same way, she agreed. And when she was invited to pray for Jesus to come into her life, she said yes and received Him.

Mary then asked the owner of the shop what she liked best about the Lifestory.

"I like it all! Can I also learn that story and share it?"

Mary assured her this would happen soon. She was excited to find such a person. I will refer to her as Mentor S.

Mary asked if she could tell the Lifestory to some of the young ladies in training. Mentor S asked her to tell them all. They all came to the Lord with a joy that filled the stitching center. They prayed a commitment prayer because they believed in the goodness of Christ. Mary encouraged them to read God's Word to learn more about Jesus.

A few days later, Mary called the shop and offered to teach the

Lifestory to Mentor S, along with any of the young ladies who were interested. Mentor S was thrilled and arranged a time. Nearly a dozen women finished the Lifestory training. Those learning a skill at the stitching center had also become a team of Lifestory tellers.

Torch to Bangalore

Mentor S invited Mary to a conference during the summer in Bangalore. The conference was on helping young women escape the circle of poverty and would involve nearly two weeks of training for young women who needed encouragement and vision. Mentor S asked Mary to be a part of the program.

Mary agreed this would be a perfect opportunity to tell the Lifestory to many who would then challenge the darkness. Conference organizers expected more than a hundred women from the suburbs of Bangalore to attend. Most of these women supplemented their income by selling things they made at home. The stitching seminar and the workshops would teach them to make cards and bags to sell to local distributors. Empowering women to take charge of their future in this manner is one way to combat human trafficking. Most important to Mary and Mentor S was telling the Lifestory to these women who needed it, who then could share the Light of the World with others.

Several of these women came to love Jesus and His word, and they learned a skill. Both were a great prize. We were all thrilled there was now a station of light in Bangalore. This new sowers team is now under Ms. Suhani's leadership. She lives in a border village and is grateful for Mentor S and Mary.

Now there are twenty eight new Lifestory tellers in Bangalore armed with the truth of God's Word and new practical skills.

The Lifestory Continues ...

The story of the Lifestory tellers is going forward.

LESSONS LEARNED

Many plain truths of scripture had become clear to us as we followed Jesus in starting movements in diverse places.

God cares for everyone He draws to Jesus, and no one can snatch them out of His hand, as it reads in John 10:29: "My Father, who has given them to Me, is greater than all; and no one is able to snatch them out of My Father's hand."

Neither Jesus nor the disciples limited their witness to those they could follow up. They focused on following God's Word, and sometimes they left the results in His hands. Consider this, according to Mark 5:18–19: "And when He got into the boat, he who had been demon possessed begged Him that he might be with Him. However, Jesus did not permit him, but said to him, 'Go home to your friends, and tell them what great things the Lord has done for you, and how He has had compassion on you."

Jesus's focus was training fishers of men. In His parable of the sower, Jesus taught these disciples that they were responsible for sowing widely, not how the soil responds (Matthew 13:1–8, 18–23; Mark 4:3–8, 14–20; Luke 8:5–8,11–15).

Under the Holy Spirit's leading, Philip led a high Ethiopian official to trust in Jesus and baptized him that day. This official then returned to his own country without any kind of follow up as to what happened with the eunuch check out this in Acts 8:39: "Now when they came up out of the water, the Spirit of the Lord caught Phillip away, so that the eunuch saw him no more; and he went on his way rejoicing."

In the Lifestory, God has given us a way for helping those most isolated from areas where the gospel is established to experience this same kind of fruitfulness. God may prefer that we engage in follow up with all we can, but He has allowed us to have room to trust Him to take over and do it.

Emergency Treatment for Sinners

Our salvation is Jesus's emergency. Our need for redemption is dire. We know this because of all Jesus left behind to come and save us. He views our situation seriously. How then should we feel toward others as we follow Him? Do we share His concern? Is the salvation of others an emergency to us? What about: "As the Father sent me, so I send you."

There are Lifestory tellers who have sacrificed their lives to see their families and communities experience the blessing of God in Jesus. We see more clearly that it is not an unreasonable thing to give up our lives, considering the importance of our mission.

It is unreasonable to just be reckless, but it is also unreasonable to ignore a simple appointment that may be arranged by God to win someone else. Letting large groups perish without introducing them to Jesus is not reasonable.

In an Islamic library, a man stood beside me. I assessed his ability to understand English. It was positive. As I have listened to Jesus in so many similar circumstances, He has taught me that I no longer need to ask the question "Should I tell him the Lifestory?" Jesus has already shown me this is why He sent that person to me. I told the Lifestory. The man trusted Jesus. It was that simple.

We may wonder, *Is this the dawn of battle, or are we just waking up to realize we are already in the middle of the battle?* I have known seven martyrs. Their families can answer without hesitation whether we are in a battle. We must put on the armor of God every day.

Jesus has given us something that works. The Lifestory movements are rapidly multiplying laborers for the harvest. It profits us to seek more worshippers of the Almighty God. I have found it a very good thing to stand quietly and listen for the voice of Jesus. Make the sacrifice and do the work.

Society cross over

CAN SOCIETY CHANGE?

It was a hot July night in Rawalpindi, Pakistan 2018. As I was walking from my hotel, I saw two street children, each small for their age, clawing through a large, overstuffed, and stinking garbage container. They were just two of several hundred doing the same in that section of the city.

They had to complete their daily quota, or they would likely have no food, no sleep, and no way to escape a beating with the hose or cane. The night was dark, and glaring headlights only sporadically illuminated the sad scene. These two must have just started, as there were only a few plastic bottles and aluminum scraps in their bags. One was flinging things aside and crying in frustration. They were two little children searching through piles of nothing, scratching out an existence on the edge of eternity.

They stirred my heart, and I asked Jesus to make me a better fisher of men. That night I shared the Lifestory over and over with people on the street. Concerned for my safety, some warned me to stop, as I was publicly mentioning Jesus. They invited me into their homes, hoping I would leave the crowded street. I could not.

Eventually, I headed back to my hotel, passing again the children and their trash bin. Stuffing a paper cup with a couple of bills and tossing it in the bin as I walked by, I reached down and pulled out a bill as if it had come from the trash.

I said to one of the digging like rats children: "Is this yours?"

One of the tortured souls clambered over and grabbed it, then tucked it in the fold of his cloth and immediately went back to work. I made it back to my room and tried to wash the garbage smell and residue off my clothes, but some of it is still there. I can feel it.

Even now I dream and pray that people in this area would be saved and save these dear little ones. My eyes are dry, but my heart is pounding like a thunderstorm. *Dear Jesus, how can we fix a society that has no compassion for such children?*

JON SMITH

REVIEWING LIFESTORY

What had been keeping their friends from coming to Jesus? The biggest barrier they could see was their constant arguments with them over everything spiritual. Something needed to change.

After much prayer, they realized they needed to focus more on Jesus and less on their disagreements. They needed to hear more directly from Jesus, as the barriers to introducing their people to God's blessing in Jesus were looming over them like a high wall.

They had thought about starting over in a new location, but became convinced it was their approach that needed to change, not their location. Rather than move to a new area, They needed a different way to introduce people to God's blessing in Jesus.

Courage to change became as important as the change itself. Both personal cost and timing factored into their decision. They were growing older at what seemed to be an increasing rate.

Jesus's example and closeness gave them the courage they needed. He is the eternal Word of God, yet He came into our world, bridging the vast difference between earth and heaven. Could they similarly bridge the cultural distance to share God's blessing of redemption through Jesus Christ?

Their outreach had been moving along at a snail's pace. By all appearances, the multitudes were ready to come to Jesus, but their close-knit groups would always pull back at the last moment. They carefully considered what questions God would have them ask Him. Praying for Him to prepare the people's hearts would be redundant because it was evident, they were already prepared. Jon and Jerri needed to have God do a work in themselves so others could receive His message. It was essential that they hear the voice of the Lord.

They were returning to India from a meeting with some trusted counselors. Jerri and Jon needed to decide about their future. It was a good time for to fast and pray. They found a hotel in Delhi with an affordable rate, so they checked in and began to fast.

Four days went by.

It was late in the night and Jon was praying and waiting. Jerri was resting, and the hotel room was dark, except for a single light. His bible and a blank sheet of paper lay on the table, waiting for his thoughts. In his mind, Jesus said, "Stop arguing."

He immediately asked, "How? They counter every important point I bring up, whether logical or not."

A little while later, He sensed God urging him to write a simple story. Jon thought about this and asked himself. What kind of story? Then he sensed that God would have him write his favorite story.

His bible was open to John 3:16. That passage contains his favorite story, so he started writing. It was difficult at first. This would have to be comprehensive, but simple enough that everybody could understand it.

He made the first part of the story short, including the essence of the Gospel in case he only had a short time with someone. Then he fit the life, death, burial, and resurrection of Jesus into one minute.

Next came the fall of Adam and Eve, in less time.

After this he searched the Bible references that relate to John three and Jesus's conversation with Nicodemus. The part that interested him most was about Moses lifting a serpent on a pole. Next to Moses parting the Red Sea, this is one of the greatest examples in history of desperate people receiving a second chance.

Jesus identifies himself with the serpent on the pole by stating He must be lifted up the same way. He equates this with being born again for. It is the way God provided an antidote for lost and suffering souls.

This part of the story proves exciting because it tells of a large group of people who made a disastrous mistake that would cost them their lives, but God made a way for each of them to individually have a second chance.

We can compare that to the curse of death we all face because of Adam's sin and our own sins. Jesus provides us with a second chance at eternal life by Him taking our place as the cursed one who was hanged on the cross to bear our iniquities.

This story reveals the nature of God, who desires to save us. This is an important part of what they want to tell everyone. They needed their story to relate to people everywhere, so Jon decided to personalize it with this question: "If you and I were there in front of Moses, we both would have looked up to that serpent on the pole rather than die, wouldn't we?"

Most people answer yes to this question. It also opens the door to the next part of the story and helps us cooperate with God as we lift up Jesus and present Him as the saviour.

After the question about the serpent, the story reviews the interaction between Jesus and Nicodemus, then ends with us asking another question: "Do you remember the part in the story where the condemned people looked up to the serpent on the pole and were saved? In the very same way, Jesus is inviting you to look up to Him and trust Him to also save you. Will you trust Jesus to save you now?"

Then he thought it is best to wait quietly as the Holy Spirit works in their heart. Next, he invites verbal prayer to accept and follow the Lord. After this he adds another question to help each new person who trusted Jesus step forward to becoming a multiplying disciple by answering this question; What did you like best about the story?

This question helps us listen to what God may be saying to them. They may say something like, I like the part about Moses and the fiery serpents.

Then Jon plans to say, I like that too. I think your answer tells me something about you. You have people in your life who you would like to also hear this same story, don't you?

Now it is time to wait for their answer, then continue. You will be happy to know there is a simple training for those who want to follow Jesus and learn to tell this story. This training is only about three hours. You can learn the story and tell this story to whomever you wish.

Then Jon would say: Let me give you my contact information. Put it in your phone now and send me a message so I know you have it right; then you can contact me anytime.

Here is an added thought and dialogue about pointing them to the Bible: You told God you will follow Jesus. Here is a way you might do this. There is a book all about Jesus and what He did while He was here on earth and in heaven. Read the bible and God will guide you in following Jesus as you read about what He said and did. Listen to Him and hear what He says. This book is available through a free app and I can help you put on your phone right now. Would you like me to help you do this?

Leave no one behind

FOLLOW JESUS?

We know how a society can change because we have begun to see such changes in communities where Lifestory movements are spreading. Part of my responsibility now is telling other believers what Jesus is doing, then inviting others to come follow Him, trusting Him to fulfill his purpose.

We can feel His deep urgency, hear His voice, and immediately follow Him and we are assured through God's Word that He will never leave us. We know we are following Him if we make His will a higher priority than our own goals and dreams. He came from the perfect kingdom to earth for one reason: to seek and to save which is lost.

In Matthew 21:33 to 41, Jesus tells the parable of the tenants. A landowner planted a vineyard, then left it in the hands of some tenant farmers. When it was time for the harvest, he sent his servants to collect his share. But the tenants beat the first servant, and killed the second, and stoned the third, and they treated the rest the same way. Last of all, the landowner sent his son, feeling that he would be respected. But the farmers, knowing that the son is the heir, and conspired to kill him too, and to steal his inheritance. Matthew 21:40 "Therefore, when the owner of the vineyard comes, what will he do to those vinedressers?" Does this represent the religious elite who were supposed to gather fruit for the lord of the vineyard? Did they do so? Can we find ourselves in this story?

Our friends in the harvest are telling us that today is the day for harvesting. Harvest now! Pick up your tools and harvest. Many new believers are now harvesting multitudes of souls in their home country for the kingdom of God. They say, "I am harvesting. Now it is your turn. Start harvesting." They dream of a great day coming. Can we all have the same dream?

If anyone has a full presentation of the Gospel they wish to use, we wish them well and encourage them to go harvest with it. If you choose to start with the Lifestory we will commit to help you. You want a movement, we will help you with that also. We will gladly share all we have learned in starting Lifestory movements and bringing in multitudes.

WITNESS TO MOVEMENT

In John 4:32, Jesus states the following: "My food is to do the will of him who sent me and to finish his work." Seeking to do God's will is good. Joining Jesus in seeking to finish His work is even better. In the same way, telling the Lifestory is good. Seeking to start a movement is even better.

Lifestory movements can only be started with a clear commitment and accountability in telling the Lifestory. Those who learn the story from us may make a higher commitment in this regard than we do.

When Coach learned about my commitment to share the Lifestory four times a day, he made the same commitment. The developing Lifestory leaders asked us how they could do better for Jesus. They learned about this commitment and embraced it as well; then they committed to tell the Lifestory with increasing frequency.

These commitments were not made privately; they were made publicly with accountability. Without such commitment, the Lifestory may never have become.

The Lifestory Team

Perhaps as you read these stories Jesus has spoken to you about family or friends who have been sitting on the fence and might benefit from a clear invitation to make a yes or no decision about following Jesus.

Maybe Jesus is sharing His heart with you regarding some lost segment of your community or even a distant place where Jesus is not yet loved and followed.

Don't settle for merely reading about how God is leading others to bear fruit in the harvest. If you are not yet personally fruitful in the harvest, set aside time to listen to Jesus about how and where He wants you to follow Him to become a fisher of men. If you are already fruitful, ask Him if there is anything He would prune from your life to make you more fruitful. Ask Him if there is any reason He would *not* want you to learn this Lifestory and share it with your loved ones and others you meet.

Starting Lifestory movements is a simple matter of listening to Jesus and try using the Lifestory to invite others to hear and follow Jesus, and offer training to those who say yes to Jesus. If Jesus is leading you this way, please let us know at LifestoryTellers777@gmail. com so we can pray for you and offer you what coaching we can.

Ten years of practical experience under the Lord's guidance has led us to discover basic essentials that make Lifestory movements particularly fruitful. At LifestoryTellers.net, we are compiling helpful resources. If you try following Jesus with the Lifestory and do not have similar results, ask Jesus for guidance, then visit us on the web.

Jesus is doing something new and wonderful through the Lifestory movements. We are indebted to the prayer and financial supporters who have been with us from the beginning and others who joined us along the way. If reading this book has stirred you to help, Please become part of our outreach. One major effort that could interest you is the challenging project of raising up the widows and orphans of Kashmir. We have found that Jesus favors giving to Widows and orphans and with the help of all the Lifestory teams in Kashmir and the support from people like yourself, we have been thrilled to see his hand of mercy reach across the obstacles of language, culture and religion by addressing the needs of the widows and orphans caught in the violence that grips the Northern Union Territory of Jammu and Kashmir. The fighting exists from the conflict between India, Pakistan and the freedom fighters of Kashmir. All are struggling to own Kashmir. You may find more about this event from the book Curfewed Night, written by a Kashmiri journalist, Basharat Peer and published by Scribner, of Simon and Schuster. It mentions something of the volume of deaths created, but the numbers of those imprisoned by India and not released in over seventy years is staggering.

The widows and orphans created from the conflict are the worst casualties of the event.

Of the three mentioned adversaries none can help the widows and orphans. They are left in squalor and assigned a slow and dishonorable death. India counts them as militants. Pakistan counts them as foreign, and freedom fighters can't be connected because of hiding their identity. With Jesus we have found them as precious in the Lord. They come to him through the servants of the Lord laboring in the harvest with the lifestory tellers. Now teams of lifestory widows and orphans lead in calling them to safety in Jesus Christ. You can join them. We have given all the help sent to us for this through Allegro Services who trust the Lord and are found on our website lifestorytellers.net/Kashmir relief.

We have given through helpers like you. For the last five years together we have fed and cared for all the needs of more than a hundred widows and much more than five hundred children every day. More widows are coming to the Lord Jesus and will soon double the amount mentioned. We are faithful and rejoice for the help of God and people like you and because of Allegro, and the publisher of this book who call on the name of the Lord. All the profit generated by the sale of this book and others to come goes directly into the funds for the widows and orphans and some reformed or innocent prisoners from the Union Territory of Jammu & Kashmir.

To share in this labor of love through your prayer or giving, visit LifestoryTellers.net select Kashmir relief.

Appendix: The Lifestory

The Lifestory has been refined through countless retellings in a wide variety of cultures to maximize its helpfulness to those the Father is drawing to Jesus.

In every training, please use the latest version without alteration at LifestoryTellers.net. You may consider scheduling a training. If you do *not* find most people saying yes to Jesus, check first with the Lord and Review the Lifestory and method, and contact us.

The Lifestory

Start with silent prayer and a smile.

I have a short story. It takes five minutes. Would you like to hear it?

Part 1: Introduction (Eighty Seconds or Less)

Hi, I have a short story it is about five minutes. Would you like to hear it?

It is 2021. Most people know that, but not many people know why.

The reason is two thousand years ago time stopped and started over again, and now it's 2021.

The important thing is, why did time stop?

According to the ancient scriptures, God saw that the hearts of everyone on earth were broken, and they could not come up to Him. So He decided to fix this problem.

God came down to earth and took on human form. He was born into the world like all of us, but while He was here He did things only God could do.

He walked on water. He healed the sick and raised the dead. But the most important thing He did was to fix our problem of brokenness and sin.

He lived a perfect life, then gathered all the mistakes of all people for all time and put them alongside His perfect life. With His great love, He exchanged his perfect life for our broken lives, took all our sin with Him down to the grave, and paid for it with His own blood.

After that, He overcame death and went up into heaven. And left the door open so everyone who follows Him can come inside. The problem is, not very many are going through this door, and that's why I tell this story.

PART 2: CREATION (GENESIS 1–3, THIRTY-FIVE SECONDS OR LESS)

When God first made the world, according to the ancient scriptures, there were no people in it, so He made two, Adam and Eve. They were very happy. And they were so close to God, like these two clasped hands.

There was just one rule: not to eat of a certain tree. But they ate from the tree and broke the rule. And they didn't just break the rule; they broke the relationship. It's no longer close anymore, it is broken and it has been that way ever since.

PART 3: MOSES (NUMBERS 21:4–9, EIGHTY-FIVE SECONDS OR LESS)

Roughly twenty-five hundred years after Adam and Eve, according to the ancient scriptures in the book of Numbers 21, this is what happened.

God called a man named Moses to lead more than a million people from Egypt to the promised land. On the way, the people did evil in the sight of God, so God struck them with fiery serpents that bit the people, and many of them died.

Some ran to Moses and said, "Please forgive us, and pray for us."

Moses prayed, and God heard his prayer:

"Moses, make a bronze serpent, put it on a pole, and hold it up in front of the people. Tell them if they have been bitten, and they look up to the serpent on the pole, they will live. If they don't, they will surely die."

And it happened just this way.

And even today, in this city and in every city in the world, you may find this symbol of a serpent on a pole on a hospital, ambulance, or pharmacy.

If the group is small, ask their name(s) here.

Now I imagine, [insert their name(s)], if you were with me in front of Moses, and we had been bitten by those serpents, we would have listened to his instructions and looked up to the serpent on the pole rather than die, wouldn't we?

If their answer is positive, say, "Good, because this has something to do with the end of the story."

PART 4: NICODEMUS (JOHN 3:1–15, SEVENTY-FIVE SECONDS OR LESS)

About fifteen hundred years after Moses, according to the ancient scriptures in the book of John Chapter three, in the New Testament, this is what happened:

It was a dark night, and there was a man in the street. His name was Nicodemus, and he was a great teacher of the law. He was looking for Jesus. When he found Jesus, Nicodemus said: "Ah-ha! I know you are from heaven because you do things only God can do."

Jesus replied, "Oh, Nicodemus, you can never see the kingdom of heaven unless you are born again!"

Nicodemus: "What? How can a person be born again? Must he go back to his mother and come from her a second time when he is old?"

Jesus said, "Truly you are a great teacher, but I have something for you. That which is flesh is flesh, but that which is Spirit is like the wind. You don't know where it's coming from, and you certainly don't know where it is going. Everyone who is born of the Spirit is just like that.

"And just as Moses lifted the serpent on the pole, so must I be lifted up that I may draw all people to myself."

PART 5: INVITATION (FORTY SECONDS OR LESS)

Now, my friend [their name], I know Jesus loves you. He doesn't want you to ever perish. He wants you to have eternal life.

So my question for you is simple: Remember how the people looked up to that serpent on the pole in the wilderness and were saved?

In the very same way, Jesus is inviting you to look up to Him and trust Him now to save you also. My question is: Yes or no?

AFTER THE STORY INVITE THEM TO TALK DIRECTLY TO GOD

Great! Now that God has touched your life, would you say a short prayer with me?

Great. Just say your name where I say mine:

"God, my name is _____."

"I ask Jesus to for forgive me and come into my life."

"I will follow Jesus." Amen.

LEAD THEM TOWARD REPRODUCING

Now I have one more question: What part of the story did you like best?

I think this tells me something about you. I think you know someone who you would like to hear this story too. Is that true?

You will be happy to know that a simple training is available for those who want to follow Jesus and learn to tell this story. This simple training is only about three hours; then you can tell this story to whomever you wish.

Let me give you my contact information. Put it in your phone now and send me a message so I know you have it right. You can contact me anytime.

LEAD THEM TOWARD FOLLOWING JESUS

You have told God you will follow Jesus. There is a great book all about Jesus and what He did while He was here on earth and in heaven. God will guide you in following Jesus as you read what He said and did. Listen to Him and hear what He says. This book can be found in a free app on your phone right now.

ABOUT THE AUTHOR

Jon Smith and his wife, Jerri, went to Asia as aid workers with a desire to share the Gospel. In 2006.

We feel this is a new age and it is time for all of us to get up and join the action. It is the greatest time. Listen to what God gave Apostle Paul for us in II Thessalonians 1:6,7&8: "since it is a righteous thing with God to repay with tribulation those who trouble you, and to give you who are troubled rest with us when the Lord Jesus is revealed from heaven with His mighty angels, in flaming fire taking vengeance on those who do not know God, and on those who do not obey the gospel of our Lord Jesus Christ."

Did you just say hooray? Wait a minute. Did God call us to love our enemies? If God called us to love our enemies shouldn't we go out and see that they get redeemed at all cost? What are we doing just waiting for the fire to come and burn them all? Should not every one of us who are called believers get up and go win every person we possibly can?

If this is true with any of us. Let's get real. Undo all the things we have fortified ourselves with to keep us from being uncomfortable including desiring that we are not called to be an evangelist.

Some could pick up the lifestory and use it. Make a goal for every day of how many we will ask per day. We could begin by saying I have a short story it is about five minutes, would you like to hear it? Then tell the lifestory or read it to them. Would it make us stronger to commit this idea to God, and at least one other person and tell them what our specific goal is?

Perhaps we could decide this and consider sometime later to start a team and work together till we can pray for your movement in an area, or a neighborhood?

Printed in the United States
by Baker & Taylor Publisher Services